Network Management
A Practical Perspective

Network Management
A Practical Perspective

Allan Leinwand

Karen Fang

ADDISON-WESLEY PUBLISHING COMPANY
Reading, Massachusetts ● Menlo Park, California ● New York
Don Mills, Ontario ● Wokingham, England ● Amsterdam ● Bonn
Sydney ● Singapore ● Tokyo ● Madrid ● San Juan ● Milan ● Paris

This book is in the **Addison-Wesley UNIX and Open Systems Series**
Series Editors: Marshall Kirk McKusick and John S. Quarterman

Many of the designations used by the manufacturers and sellers to distinguish their
products are claimed as trademarks. Where those designations appear in this book,
and Addison-Wesley was aware of a trademark claim, the designations have been
printed in initial caps or all caps.

The programs and applications presented in this book have been included for their
instructional value. They have been tested with care, but are not guaranteed for any
particular purpose. The publisher does not offer any warranties or representations,
nor does it accept any liabilities with respect to the programs or applications.

Library of Congress Cataloging-in-Publication Data
Leinwand, Allan.
    Network management: a practical perspective/Allan Leinwand,
Karen Fang.
        p.   cm.
    Includes bibliographical references and index.
    ISBN 0–201–52771–5
    1. Computer networks—Management.   I. Fang, Karen.
II. Title.
TK5105.5.L398   1993   92-2258
004.6—dc20   CIP

1 2 3 4 5 6 7 8 9 10-HA-95949392

To our family and friends

Series Foreword

Marshall Kirk McKusick
John S. Quarterman

Addison-Wesley is proud to publish the **UNIX and Open Systems Series.** The primary audience for the Series will be system designers, implementors, administrators and their managers. The core of the series will consist of books detailing operating systems, standards, networking, and programming languages. The titles will interest specialists in these fields, as well as appeal more broadly to computer scientists and engineers who must deal with open-systems environments in their work. The Series comprises professional reference books and instructional texts.

Open systems allow users to move their applications between systems easily; thus, purchasing decisions can be made on the basis of cost-performance ratio and vendor support, rather than on which systems will run a user's application suite. Decreasing computer hardware prices have facilitated the widespread adoption of capable multiprocess, multiuser operating systems, UNIX being a prime example. Newer operating systems, such as Mach and Chorus, support additional services, such as lightweight processes. The Series illuminates the design and implementation of all such open systems. It teaches readers how to write applications programs to run on these systems, and gives advice on administration and use.

The Series treats as a unified whole the previously distinct field of networking and operating systems. Networks permit open systems to share hardware and software resources, and allow people to communicate efficiently. The exponential growth of networks such as the Internet, and the adoption of protocols such as TCP/IP in industry, government, and academia, have made network and system administration critically important to many organizations. This series will examine many aspects of network protocols, emphasizing the interaction with operating systems. It will focus on the evolution in computer environments, and will assist professions in the development and use of practical networking technologies.

Standards for programming interfaces, protocols, and languages are a key concern as networks of open systems expand within organizations and across the globe. Standards can be useful for system engineering, application programming, marketing, and procurement; but standards that are released too late, cover too little, or are too narrowly defined can be counterproductive. This series will encourage its readers to participate in the standards process by presenting material detailing the use of specific standards to write application programs, and to build modern multiprocess, multiuser computing environments.

Newer operating systems are implemented in object-oriented languages, and network protocols use specialized languages to specify data formats and to compile protocol descriptions. As user interfaces become increasingly sophisticated, the level at which they are programmed continues to evolve upward, from the system-call level to remote-procedure-call compilers and generic graphic user-interface–description environments. The effects of new languages on systems, programs, and users are explored in this series.

Preface

What is Network Management? Probably anyone who has had contact with a data network has a different conception of the subject. Depending on the size and complexity of the data network, this form of management could be as simple as having one person check the PCs on the local area network once a week or as involved as having a staff of 50 people armed with beepers and protocol analyzers on 24-hour call. From one network to another, priorities can differ dramatically.

We hope this book will help the network engineer obtain a clearer view of network management in his or her individual environment. Because network engineers can have different viewpoints of network management, our first goal in writing the book has been to define all the pieces that make up network management. We have used real-world examples and applications to introduce the engineer to each of the five categories of network management as defined by the International Organization for Standardization Open Systems Interconnection (ISO OSI) Network Management Forum. These categories are fault management, configuration management, performance management, security management, and accounting management.

We also wanted to provide the engineer with a practical means of designing and/or evaluating a network management system for his or her particular networking environments. Accordingly, for each category of network management, we offer descriptions of simple, complex, and advanced tools from which the engineer can use depending on the needs of their organization. Although we realize that some of these tools might not exist today, we included them because an engineer could determine that a particular functionality would be useful and might decide to pursue its development.

In the last chapters of the book, we explore further into the process of network management. We tell the engineer how to get information from the network through the use of network management protocols and offer some of the "bells and whistles"—additional productivity tools that can help make a network engineer's life easier. Finally, we take a close look at the information that is available from many network devices on the market today via MIB-II.

We would like to thank the following people for their generous support in the form of time spent reviewing the materials in this book and valuable suggestions on how to make it work for the network engineer:

Daniel Blum
Takoma Park, MD

Smoot Carl-Mitchell
Texas Internet Consulting

Lee Damon
IBM TJ Watson Research Center

Jeri Dansky
Hewlett-Packard

Eric Decker
Cisco Systems

John Gong
Oracle Corporation

Allan Hastings
AT&T Bell Laboratories

Brian Jemes
Hewlett-Packard

Michael J. Karels
University of California, Berkeley

Cheryl Krupczak
GA Institute of Technology

George Leach
AT&T Paradyne

Doug McCallum
Sunsoft

Paul Ressler
BBN Communications

Sven Sampson
Hewlett-Packard

Randy Strickfaden
Hewlett-Packard

Kean Stump
University Computing Services
Oregon State University

John S. Quarterman
Texas Internet Consulting

If you have any comments or questions with regard to network management or this book and would like to contact us, you can reach Allan via electronic mail at leinwand@cisco.com and Karen at fang@cisco.com. You can also reach both of us via the Cisco System's main telephone number: (415) 326–1941.

Menlo Park, California   A. L.
                                                                         K. F.

Contents

1

Overview of Network Management

In this chapter:
- Definition of a data network
- Benefits of a data network
- Role of the network engineer
- Basic steps in implementing a data network
- Definition of network management
- Overview of the five components of network management
- Methods of designing a network management system
- Examples of network management systems

*The first sight Chris saw that morning was at least one hundred yellow notes stuck to the terminal, the answering machine message light blinking out of control and a line of people surrounding the office space. In unison they all groaned, "**The network is down!**"*

Thus starts another day in the life of a network engineer. Chris flew past the people and started typing furiously on a keyboard. Sure enough, there was no access to Chicago, Singapore, New York, San Francisco or Paris. Major portions of MegaNet, *the company wide international network, seemed to have disappeared into a black hole. Chris sighed and glanced at the "Don't Panic" button stuck to the wall. In the direction of the customer service group a faint voice was heard saying, "... I'm sorry, can you call back later, the computer is down...". To the right, the order processing department was involved in a rousing game of bridge as they waited to input orders to the computer at Corporate. The Research and Development department chair races originally scheduled for five P.M. were in full swing. It seemed like the only people concerned were Chris and the upper management crowding around the office.*

1

Chris immediately knew how the day would proceed: isolate the problem, fix the problem, and print out copious reports and graphs for management showing what happened and why it will not happen again. And with a little bit of luck, maybe even a cup of coffee to drink. Before grabbing a screwdriver and heading for the computer room, Chris added another yellow note to the pile on the computer screen which said, "Investigate network management systems—ASAP!"

This is a familiar scenario to many people. Data networks have become common and accepted in our daily lives, although we may not always be aware of them. For example, they allow us 24-hour access to our bank accounts and enable retail stores to approve our credit card purchases immediately. Research and development centers use data networks to keep abreast of rapidly changing technologies, while companies of all sizes rely on them to perform necessary day-to-day business operations.

The importance of data networks lies in their ability to provide exceptionally rapid and efficient access to vast quantities of information. We have come to depend on data networks so much that disruption of a network can mean disruption of business and/or our daily lives, resulting in, for example, frustrated users and/or customers, delays in receipt of critical data, possible loss of business revenue, or inability to reach much-needed funds when the bank is closed. Therefore keeping a data network in good working order is critical. This is where data network management comes in.

In this chapter, we define a data network and briefly describe how to implement one. We introduce the network engineer as a key player in creating and managing networks. Next, we present the concept of network management and briefly describe its five components—fault management, configuration management, security management, performance management, and accounting management—which form the bulk of discussion in this book. Last, we discuss possible designs of network management systems and offer you some examples of such systems.

1.1 Definition of a Data Network

A *data network* is a collection of devices and circuits that can provide a means for transferring data from one computer to another. It enables users at different locations to share the resources of a larger computer stationed elsewhere.

Most people come in contact with a data network everyday and never realize it. A well-known example of a data network is the automated teller machine, or ATM. An ATM processes bank and credit card transactions such as your withdrawal of money from your checking account or your request for a cash advance on a credit card. However, ATMs are usually operated at *remote sites,* that is, at locations separate from (remote from) the main computer that contains the information about your accounts. They therefore do not possess the full computing power that the main computer does; to do so would be redundant and costly. Instead, an ATM uses a data network to establish a communication link between it and the main computer, thus enabling the ATM to share the computing resources offered by that machine. The ATM uses this link to send information about your transaction, such as the account number and the amount to be withdrawn or advanced, to the main computer, which in turn checks your account to ensure you have sufficient funds or available credit line to cover the withdrawal or advance. Assuming you do, the computer then sends along the communication link the necessary signals that trigger the ATM to dispense your money (see Fig. 1.1).

In another example, a scientist at a research lab in Chicago wants to run a program. The local lab computer will take eight hours to complete it. However, that local computer also is connected via a data network to a supercomputer in Miami, which can run the program in only three hours. In this case, using a data network to access the supercomputer would save five hours of computing time and enable the scientist to have the program results much quicker.

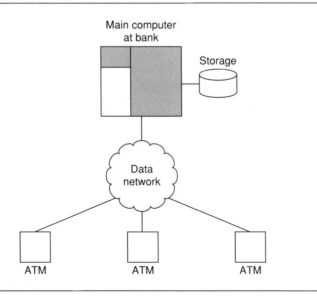

FIGURE 1.1
The data network provides the communication link between the bank's main computer and the ATMs.

As you can see, linking computers via a data network allows organizations to share the information resources of other computers, thus helping those organizations become more efficient and productive.

1.2 Role of the Network Engineer

Because of the importance of a functioning data network, one or more computer system experts called *network engineers* usually are made responsible for installing, maintaining, and troubleshooting the network. For the network engineer, the solution to a network problem could be simple, such as answering a confused user's question, or more complicated, such as replacing failed or malfunctioning equipment or initiating disaster recovery procedures due to a catastrophic event.

Further, as a network expands, the size and number of potential problems also increase, as does the scope and complexity of the network engineer's job. To accomplish their task, engineers need to know large amounts of information about the data network. The sheer volume of this information can quickly become unmanageable, particularly as the network grows and changes. To help the engineers do their jobs, the concept of network management evolved.

We define and present an overview of network management in Section 1.4 and then devote Chapters 2 through 7 to a detailed discussion of its components and implementation. But first, let's review the basics of how to implement a data network.

1.3 Implementation of a Data Network

Implementing a data network does not automatically guarantee that all people in an organization will be able to share computing resources. First and foremost, the data network must meet the organization's communication needs. To achieve this, the engineer must develop a comprehensive plan.

As an analogy to demonstrate why a plan is necessary, consider the highway system of the United States. Suppose the highways were not sponsored by the government. Instead, each town or city with citizens that wished to travel to another town or city would have to build a highway between the two sites. Obviously, within a very short time the road system would be quite a mess. Each highway would have a specific purpose, but would not necessarily contribute to an effective overall highway scheme. As you can imagine, management of this road system would be quite complicated, if not impossible. Fortunately, the government has dictated the (somewhat) logical planning, architecture, and building of the nation's major highways, usually with the goal of providing access between metropolitan areas.

Just as highway engineers work to provide roadways to help the typical driver, the network engineer works to produce a data network that satisfies the needs of the typical user of a computer system. Obviously, a thorough analysis of these users' requirements regarding that system will heavily influence the design plan of the data network.

When developing a plan, network engineers will often survey the user community to help them provide a useful setup. The design may include adding new pieces to an existing network to give access to new locations, providing redundancy to guard against isolation given the failure of a single circuit, or increasing the bandwidth of a network link. Also, many times part of the process incorporates an examination of the applications and protocols that will utilize the network.

Once a network plan is developed, the engineer should perform the following tasks to implement the data network:

1. Build
2. Maintain
3. Expand
4. Optimize
5. Troubleshoot

First, the engineer, using the network plan, should determine what is needed to build the network, that is, the required pieces of software and hardware and the desired connectivity.

Two main types of technology provide communication connectivity between points on a data network: the local area network (LAN) and the wide area network (WAN).

A *LAN* ties together hosts at speeds ranging from 4 to 100 Mbps (megabits per second) with the goal of providing connectivity over relatively short distances. A *WAN* usually operates at speeds ranging from 9.6 Kbps (kilobits per second) to 45 Mbps and beyond to provide connectivity over relatively long distances. Also, many engineers elect to build networks that use WAN technology to interconnect LANs transparently to a user of the data network.

After building the network, the network engineer next will need to maintain the network. Regardless of how much care the engineer has taken while building the network, it still will need maintaining. For example, software running on devices may change, pieces of the network will require upgrades, or equipment will develop faults and need replacing.

Changes in users' needs usually will affect the overall network plan, thus triggering the third task for the engineer: providing for expansion. Because expansion of the existing network is often preferable to redesigning and building an entirely new one, the engineer needs to apply the correct networking solution to accommodate these changes.

The fourth task of the network engineer is to optimize the data network—no simple task. Considering that a typical network may have hundreds of different devices, each with its own peculiarities and all of which must work together in harmony, only through careful planning can the engineer ensure these devices contribute optimally to a well-functioning data network. For example, the announcement of a new product or technology may lead to replacing an existing piece of equipment with a new device expected to provide better network service. The engineer would need to plan the deployment of this device carefully. Knowing which parameters on the device need setting and which are irrelevant to the existing situation, the engineer can achieve optimum network performance.

By performing each of the above steps, the network engineer can help minimize network troubles. Of course, because no network is infallible, problems will occur regardless of how well the network is managed. Therefore the need for the fifth task—troubleshooting—will always exist due to unforseen events.

1.4 Overview of Network Management

Organizations invest significant amounts of time and money building complex data networks that need to be maintained. Rather than a company's dedicating one or more network engineers to maintenance alone, it would be more cost-effective if the system could look out for itself for the most part and, in the process, perform routine tasks for the engineer. This arrangement would free the engineer to work on the future development of the network.

From this need was born the concept of network management. *Network management* is the process of controlling a complex data network so as to maximize its efficiency and productivity. Depending on the capabilities of the system that administers network management, the process will usually include collecting data—either automatically or through an engineer's manual efforts—processing that data, and then presenting it to the engineer for use in operating the network. It may also involve analyzing the data and offering solutions and possibly even handling a situation without ever bothering the engineer. It further will usually include generating reports useful to the engineer in administering the network. To accomplish all of this, network management consists of the following five functional areas:

1. Fault management
2. Configuration management
3. Security management
4. Performance management
5. Accounting management

These five areas were defined by the International Organization for Standards (ISO) Network Management forum. We discuss each briefly below and in more detail in Chapters 2 through 6.

FAULT MANAGEMENT

Fault management is the process of locating problems, or faults, on the data network. It involves the following steps:

1. Discover the problem
2. Isolate the problem
3. Fix the problem (if possible)

Using fault management techniques, the network engineer can locate and solve problems more quickly than could be done without them.

For example, in a typical setup, a user is logged into a remote system by way of several network devices. Suddenly, the connection is severed. The user reports the problem to you, the network engineer. You would begin by isolating the problem. Without an effective fault management tool, you first would want to determine whether the problem results from a user error, such as entering an invalid command or trying to access an unreachable system. If you find that no user error was involved, you then would have to check each device between the user and the remote system, beginning with the device closest to the user. Let's say you find no connectivity on this first device, as shown in Fig. 1.2. Entering the data center, you find that all the lights on the device are off. Upon investigating further, you notice signs of construction in the area and that the plug for the device is out of the wall. You conclude that someone must have unplugged the device accidentally. After reinserting the plug, this time into a wall outlet away from the construction area, you then would verify that the device now is working normally.

With the aid of a fault management tool, you could have isolated the problem much more quickly. In fact, with such a tool, you may have been able to isolate and fix the problem before the user reported it. We discuss fault management in greater detail in Chapter 2.

CONFIGURATION MANAGEMENT

The configuration of certain network devices controls the behavior of the data network. *Configuration management* is the process of finding and setting up (configuring) these critical devices.

Assume that version A of the software in an Ethernet bridge has some quirk that is causing network performance problems. To fix the anomaly, the bridge

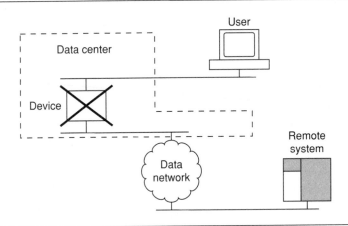

FIGURE 1.2
An effective fault management tool can help the network engineer isolate a
problem that results from a failed device on the data network.

manufacturer has released a software upgrade, version B, that will require your
installing new firmware in each of the one hundred bridges on the network.
Accordingly, you have planned a phased deployment to bring all the bridges
on the network to version B. First, however, you would need to determine the
current software version installed at each bridge. To do this without an effective
configuration management tool, you would have to physically inspect each
bridge.

A configuration management tool, however, could provide a list of all
bridges showing you the current software version for each, thus making it easier
for you to locate which need new software (see Fig. 1.3). We discuss configuration management thoroughly in Chapter 3.

SECURITY MANAGEMENT

Security management is the process of controlling access to information on the
data network. Some information stored by computers attached to the network
may be inappropriate for all users to view. Called *sensitive information,* this
information may include, for example, details about a company's new product
or its customer base.

Suppose an organization decides to employ security management techniques to allow remote access to its network via dialup lines on a terminal server
for a group of engineers, as seen in Fig. 1.4. Once engineers connect to the
terminal server, they can login to their computer to do their work.

Configuration management information	
Bridge name	Software version
Corporate 1	A
Site 23	B
Site 62	B
Corporate 8	A
•	•
•	•
•	•
•	•
•	•

FIGURE 1.3
A configuration management tool can help the network engineer determine
which software versions are installed on the data network.

After a few weeks, the administrator of one of the payroll computers on
the network comes to you with a report showing many unsuccessful remote
login attempts originating from the terminal server in use by the engineers. The
terminal server does allow access to any computer on the network—leaving the
destination host security preventing the access to sensitive information. Thus,
no engineers have gained access to the payroll computer, but the mere fact that
someone is trying is a security concern.

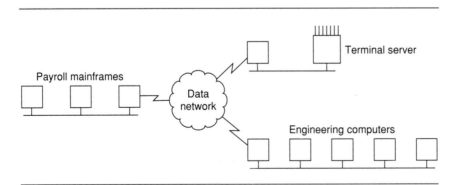

FIGURE 1.4
A security management tool allows the network engineer to monitor which
computers the users on the terminal server are attempting to access.

The first step you may take is to use a configuration management tool to limit the computer's accessibility from the terminal server. However, to discover who is attempting to gain access to this payroll computer, you will have to periodically login to the terminal server and record which engineers are using it. Hopefully, you can correlate the times at which the unsuccessful remote login attempts are being made with who is logged in on the terminal server.

Security management would give you a way to monitor the access points on the terminal server and record which engineer is using the device on a periodic basis. Security management also could provide you with audit trails and sound alarms to alert you of potential security breaches. We discuss security management in more depth in Chapter 4.

PERFORMANCE MANAGEMENT

Performance management involves measuring the performance of network hardware, software, and media. The activity that is measured may be, for example, overall throughput, percentage utilization, error rates, or response time. Using performance management information, the engineer can ensure the network will have the capacity to accommodate the users' needs.

Suppose, for example, a user complains about poor file transfer performance to a site across the network. Without a performance management tool, you would first have to look for network faults. Let's assume you find no fault. Your next step would be to evaluate the performance of each link and device between the user's terminal and the destination across the network. Let's say that during your investigation, you discover that the average utilization of one link is very close to its capacity. You might then decide that the solution to the file transfer performance problem is to upgrade the current link or install a new one to add capacity (see Fig. 1.5).

If you had a performance management tool available, you might have been able to detect early on that the link was nearing capacity, perhaps even before the performance was impacted. We present performance management in greater detail in Chapter 5.

ACCOUNTING MANAGEMENT

Accounting management involves tracking each individual and group user's utilization of network resources so that the engineer can better ensure users are provided the quantity of resources they need. It also involves granting or removing permission for access to the network.

Let's suppose you need to upgrade a department file server's network interface because its capacity to process packets is nearly maximized. Without an accounting management tool, you would not know which users have clients

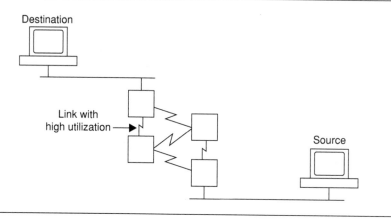

FIGURE 1.5
A performance management tool can help the network engineer find a link utilization problem between the source and destination machines.

that access the file server. Thus, you ask the users to see who has client computers that access the file server on a regular basis. As a result of your investigation, you discover that the departmental documentation group has many clients who use a desktop publishing system on the file server. After some rudimentary analysis, you conclude that this traffic contributes nearly half of the load on the file server's network interface.

You might decide that providing this documentation group with its own file server would alleviate a large amount of the network traffic that this interface card has to handle, thus removing the need to upgrade the interface card and allowing the rest of the department to remain unchanged. Further, you might decide to locate the new file server on the same network segment as the documentation group, which could reduce network traffic throughout the department.

With an accounting management tool, however, you would learn quickly that the documentation group accesses the file server with many clients on a regular basis—so you would be able to handle the situation sooner (see Fig. 1.6). We explore accounting management further in Chapter 6.

THE NETWORK MANAGEMENT PROTOCOLS

We briefly mention here that an essential step in achieving the goals of network management is to acquire information about the network. To accomplish this, a standardized set of network management protocols has been developed to help

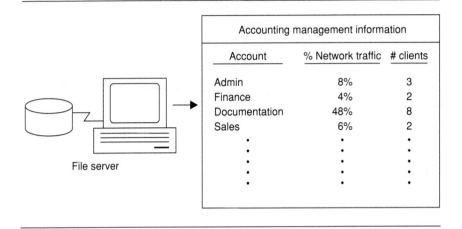

Accounting management information		
Account	% Network traffic	# clients
Admin	8%	3
Finance	4%	2
Documentation	48%	8
Sales	6%	2
.	.	.
.	.	.
.	.	.
.	.	.

File server

FIGURE 1.6
An account management tool can help the network engineer determine the dominant file server user.

extract the necessary information from all network devices. Chapter 7 provides an in-depth look at these protocols.

1.5 Definition of a Network Management System

A *network management system* is a bundle of software designed to significantly improve network efficiency and productivity. Although the network engineer can perform manually the same services that a network management system can, it is preferable that the software perform these routine tasks, thus freeing up the engineer to work on sophisticated network issues. Because a network management system is expected to accomplish many tasks simultaneously, it must have enough computing power. A common platform employed is a desktop workstation that uses a graphical window interface such as the X11 window system.

BENEFITS OF A NETWORK MANAGEMENT SYSTEM

Network management systems can help network engineers who work in many different environments.

Consider, for example, the network engineer who works in a university lab. This network may have 10 machines connected via a LAN, an environment small enough where one engineer can know all aspects of the network intimately and can deploy, maintain, and monitor it single-handedly. Still, a network management system could help this engineer in a variety of ways. The system could perform complex analysis and examine trends in traffic patterns. It could find network users who break the rules and thus cause security concerns. Further, it could find misconfigured systems and help isolate trouble areas. With a network management system performing these duties, the engineer would have more time to make the network more responsive to users' demands and needs and to accomplish projects that had been put off because of insufficient time.

Now let's look at a significantly more complex data network. A widespread version with nodes in North America, Europe, the Far East, and Australia, it might run several networking protocols, such as IBM SNA (System Network Architecture), Xerox XNS (Xerox Network Service), Appletalk, TCP/IP (Transmission Control Protocol/Internet Protocol), and DECnet. The hosts on this network might number several thousand and include workstations, minicomputers, and personal computers, along with a few other assorted devices.

It would be unreasonable to expect one person (or even a small team of people) to be able to effectively control and maintain all of these devices. A network of this size requires the management of both LAN and WAN devices, and the engineer must be able to deal with all of them. The added need to tie together the machines at all the various locations, when each location may have its own complex LAN, further complicates the engineer's job.

However, the significant difference between this environment and that of the university lab is the addition of the WAN devices, which in the latter environment would probably range from the simple to the complex. For example, a relatively simple device in the scope of wide area networking is the digital high-speed modem *DSU/CSU* (Digital Service Unit/Customer Service Unit), while a router that understands and utilizes both LAN and WAN protocols is an example of a complex network device. With many of these devices in place, the engineer must rely on the network management system to track the large volume of vital information required to determine the network's health.

Further, a network management system can perform more than just routine tasks. As an aid to finding problems, it can continuously monitor the network. Also, it can produce logs of network information and then use this information to study and analyze the network. These are tasks that could not be performed as fast and efficiently by network engineers.

In summary, in both the networking environments we described above, the concept and functionality of the network management systems are essentially identical. A more complex environment will usually require the system to perform more tasks and help the network engineer at a more sophisticated level; however, for data networks of any size, a network management system can enable engineers to work more efficiently toward customizing the network to suit users' needs.

THE ARCHITECTURE OF A NETWORK MANAGEMENT SYSTEM

Building a network management system that incorporates all the functionality necessary to provide complete management is a complex task. Software engineers working on the system must understand and meet the needs of network engineers. Ideally, they would start by designing an architecture for the system. Once that architecture was in place, the software engineers then would need to build a set of applications or tools to help the network engineer accomplish network management.

No specific rules apply to the architecture of a network management system. However, considering all the functions required of such a system, the following guidelines should be considered to realize a complete solution:

- The system must provide a graphical interface that can produce a hierarchical view of the network and allow logical connections between the various levels of the hierarchy. It needs to understand links in hierarchy and how they relate to the network's performance and functionality. A graphical interface fits well into a hierarchical structure, as network maps can be drawn to display the currently known network topology.

- The system must provide a relational database that can store and retrieve any information required by an application. Many network management applications will need to use this type of database. In particular, the system could not accomplish configuration management and accounting management effectively without it. This information can be kept in a centralized location and provide either historical or current data.

- The system must provide a means of gathering information from all relevant network devices, ideally through the use of a single network management protocol.

- The system must be easy to expand and customize. No single network management system can be built to accommodate every network by default. The system must facilitate the addition of applications and features required by a network engineer.

- The system must have a method for tracking outstanding problems or issues. As the network grows in size and complexity, this application will be invaluable. We examine in Chapter 9 how a trouble tracking system can help in network management.

POSSIBLE NETWORK MANAGEMENT SYSTEM ARCHITECTURES

Three methods concerning how to build a valid network management architecture currently prevail. The first involves building a centralized system that manages the entire network. The second deals with building a system that is distributed throughout the network. A third method combines the first two into a hierarchical system.

A centralized architecture features one large system running the majority of the desired applications (see Fig. 1.7). Each application running on the management system would store information in the same database on the central machine.

A distributed architecture calls for several peer network management systems to be running simultaneously on the data network (see Fig. 1.8). Under this setup, each system could manage, for example, a specific part of the network, as in the case of a large worldwide network where one system might manage the United States, another, Europe, and a third, the Far East. However, distributing the architecture geographically would not be required because different systems instead could manage specific types of network devices. Note, however, that although this method distributes the systems processing, a centralized database is often beneficial for information storage.

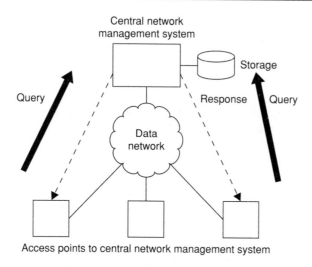

FIGURE 1.7
A central network management system receives queries from and sends responses to access points throughout the data network.

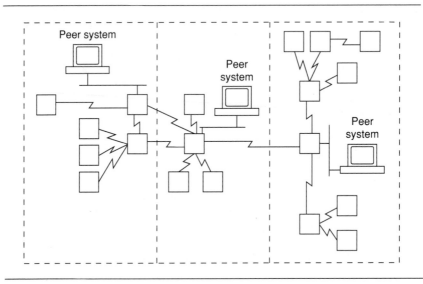

FIGURE 1.8
A data network divided into three regions. Each region is managed by a peer network management system.

A third possible architecture combines the centralized and distributed methods into a hierarchical system. The main central system from the centralized approach would still exist as the root of the hierarchy, accumulating all the essential information and allowing access from all parts of the network. Then, by setting up peer systems from the distributed architecture, this central system could delegate network management tasks that function as children in the hierarchy. This combination of methods is powerful and provides many flexible alternatives for constructing a network management system architecture.

Ideally, the architecture would reflect the structure of the organization using it. If most of an organization's administration is centralized at one location, a centralized network management system may make the most sense. On the other hand, if an organization is widely distributed with many equal levels of management, the distributed approach may be better.

Summary

Chris spent the morning finishing the reports on the major network outage which occurred a few weeks ago. In the process of clearing the computer screen of the omnipresent yellow notes, one fluttered down and landed on the floor. Scrawled on the note was, "Investigate network management systems— ASAP!"

Seeing as how MegaNet *seemed to be relatively stable and there were no fires to fight at this exact moment, Chris decided to do just that. Reaching over and grabbing a few magazines from the top of the in-tray, the network engineer settled down to read about network management.*

Hours later, Chris realized that there was more to network management than just turning things red or green on a screen.

Data networks help us perform our jobs efficiently, give us easier access to money and goods, and provide information to all aspects of society. Both private and public organizations use data networks for the transfer of information.

Because of the increasing importance and complexity of data networks, many organizations employ experts in data network management, called network engineers, to be specifically responsible for them. These engineers implement the data network—that is, build, maintain, expand, optimize, and troubleshoot it—and must know about both LAN and WAN technologies when performing these steps.

Once a data network is in place, it must be managed efficiently to maximize its potential. This is done through a process called network management, which consists of five functional areas: fault management, configuration management, security management, performance management, and accounting management. A network management system is a set of software that, through a well-defined architecture, performs network management duties. The system must have the necessary functionality to help network engineers perform their jobs in all areas of network management. The architecture of a network management system can vary, but most often organizations implement a centralized, distributed, or combined hierarchical approach.

For Further Study

Alder, J., *Bits and Bytes —The Challenge of Network Management,* Data Communications Magazine, December 1990.

Stallings, W., *Local Networks: An Introduction,* Macmillan Publishing Company, New York, 1984.

Stallings, W., *Data and Computer Communications,* Macmillan Publishing Company, New York, 1985.

Tannenbaum, A., *Computer Networks,* Prentice-Hall, Englewood Cliffs, New Jersey, 1981.

2

Fault Management

In this chapter:
- Definition of fault management
- Benefits of the fault management process
- Methods for gathering system data
- Techniques for deciding which faults to manage
- Examples of fault management tools
- Impact of faults on the network
- Flow charts of fault management tools
- Ways of reporting faults

Fault management is the process of locating and correcting network problems, which are also called *faults*. Of the many tasks involved in network management, comprehensive fault management is probably the most important. It consists of

- identifying the occurrence of a fault on the data network,
- isolating the cause of the fault, and
- correcting the fault (if possible).

In this chapter, we explore the benefits of fault management and discuss the three steps involved in accomplishing it for a data network. We describe three possible tools, from simple to advanced, that you can use and explain the methods available for a fault management system to report faults.

2.1 Benefits of the Fault Management Process

The primary benefit of fault management is that it increases network reliability by giving the network engineer tools to quickly detect problems and initiate recovery procedures. This is important because to do their jobs effectively, many people rely as heavily on a data network as they do on a telephone network. Users usually expect both to be available to them continuously, yet it is unrealistic to expect either network to function without problems or down-time. When a data network goes down, it is the job of the network engineer to maintain at least the *illusion* of complete and continuous connectivity between the users and the network. Doing this helps reinforce the reliability of the system in the eyes of users.

Unfortunately, engineers on many data networks spend too much time "fire fighting," that is, fixing one crisis after another. While managing a network in this manner may keep it going in the short run, it leaves no time for improvements. Fault management offers a variety of tools to provide the necessary information about the network's current state. Ideally, these tools can pinpoint exactly when a problem occurs and relay that information immediately to the engineer, who then can begin to work on the fault and possibly solve it without users ever becoming aware it existed. Using fault management to break the cycle of one disaster after another will increase the effectiveness of a network as well as the productivity of its engineer.

2.2 Accomplishing Fault Management

Fault management is a three-step process:

1. Identify the fault.
2. Isolate the cause of the fault.
3. Correct the fault if possible.

To illustrate, consider a DECnet node named *Cheers* that has only a single connection between it and the main data network (see Fig. 2.1). One day, this connection fails. The first thing a network management system should tell you is that a problem exists, in this case, that *Cheers* is no longer reachable. The tool next should isolate the cause of the problem—that *Cheers* is not reachable because the serial line connection from the node to the rest of the network has failed. And third, the tool should help you correct the problem, if possible. In our example, it could correct it by setting up another link between *Cheers* and the data network. As you can see, fault management, properly implemented, could correct a problem with no significant downtime.

Obviously, the first task—identifying a problem—depends on your know-ing when a problem exists. Next, you need to know if an identified problem is one you want to worry about, that is, you need to decide the most important problem to concern yourself with; not all problems will have the same priority. We discuss these two aspects of fault management next.

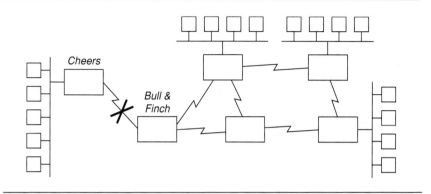

FIGURE 2.1
The single connection from *Cheers* to the main data *Bull & Finch* network has failed.

GATHERING INFORMATION TO IDENTIFY A PROBLEM

To learn that a problem exists, we need to gather data regarding the state of the network. We can use either or, preferably, both of the following methods: logging critical network events or occasionally polling network devices. Let's consider each of these methods in turn.

1. Data pertaining to critical network events are transmitted by a network device when a fault condition occurs. A *critical network event* is, for example, the failure of a link, the restart of a device, or the lack of response from a host. In most cases, relying solely on such events will not provide all the information necessary for effective fault management. For example, if a network device fails completely, it would not be able to send an event. Thus fault management tools that rely solely on critical network events may not always have the up-to-date status of every network device.

2. Occasional polling of network devices can help find faults in a timely manner. However, there is a tradeoff using this method: You must weigh the degree of timeliness you want in finding problems versus the consumption of bandwidth involved; that is, the shorter the notification time desired, the greater amount of bandwidth that probably will be consumed. Other factors to consider when deciding on a polling interval are the number of devices you want to poll and the bandwidth of the links.

For example, let's assume that each query and response is 100 bytes long, including data and header information. For a network of 30 devices, you would send 100 bytes for the query and receive 100 bytes for the response for each of our devices. This would give a total of 6000 bytes ((100 bytes + 100 bytes) * 30 devices) or 48,000 bits (6000 bytes * 8 bits/byte) of bandwidth used for each polling interval. Polling every 60 seconds would average 800 bits/second (48,000 bits/60 seconds) of bandwidth and enable you to have up-to-the-minute status of each device. Over an hour, this means 172,800,000 bits (48,000 bits * 60 seconds * 60 polls), or approximately 173 megabits of bandwidth are used for polling. Depending on the bandwidth available on the network, this may or may not be significant overhead. You could lengthen the polling interval to every 10 minutes, which would result in 17,280,000 bits (48,000 bits * 60 seconds * 6 polls), or about one-tenth the bandwidth. However, doing this means an event could occur and you might not be informed for up to 10 minutes.

A protocol that simply verifies that a device is operational also can be used to poll devices. ICMP Echo and Echo Reply (ping), Appletalk Echo, Banyan Vines Echo, and SDLC Receiver Ready (RR) frames are examples of such protocols. Note that this method by itself provides information only to help isolate a fault.

DECIDING WHICH FAULTS TO MANAGE

Not all faults will have the same priority. Some you will want to know about; others you may want the system to handle without telling you or to ignore completely. You need to decide which faults must be managed, that is, the most important types of faults for your particular network environment.

You want to do this for several reasons. First, if the number of faults is high you simply might not be able to handle the volume. Second, by limiting event traffic you can reduce the transmission of redundant or useless information and minimize the waste of network bandwidth. Consider for example the case of a workstation manufacturer who decides to generate a network event whenever a user logs on to the system. While this event provides useful information for accounting, it is irrelevant for fault management. Now suppose a department within an organization buys one hundred of these workstations. The administrators of the workstations configure them not only with a default configuration, but also with instructions to send to the central fault management tool all network events, which includes every time a user logs on to one of the new workstations. These extraneous events could quickly fill up the database on the network management system. Additionally, the bandwidth used to send this information could better be used to carry actual user data. The solution: Enable the network engineer to configure each network device to generate a specific subset of valid events. If this is not possible, then the network management system needs a way to filter the incoming events and only alert the network engineer of specific events.

Your determination of which faults to manage will be influenced by the following factors:

- The scope of control you have over the network, which will affect the amount of information you can obtain from network devices
- The size of the network

On many networks, a central organization manages the network backbone, as shown in Fig. 2.2. This backbone may consist of a variety of devices, such as X.25 switches, IP routers, and bridges. The central organization manages the critical network events for each of the backbone devices—those that may affect the entire network—thus freeing up the local administration to manage only those faults on their particular hosts and devices.

The size of the data network also will influence your decision. On a relatively small data network of, say, fewer than fifty devices, a network engineer may be able to manage every fault, including those dealing with hosts, routers, bridges, repeaters, and so forth. On a medium-sized network, the engineer may be able to manage only those faults involving critical events for each host and network device. On a large data network, the engineer may have time to examine only the critical events on the most important hosts and network devices.

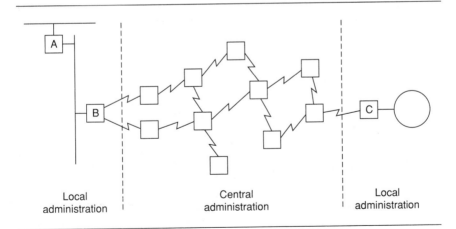

FIGURE 2.2
In this setup, the dotted line divides local and central administration of the data network. The different administrations may choose to examine different critical network events.

The Simple Network Management Protocol (SNMP) defines seven critical faults that can provide a starting point for obtaining information from the data network. (Note, however, that more information on other faults, such as printer or disk drive failure, may be necessary to manage a network.) We explore these seven faults further in Chapter 7.

2.3 Fault Management on a Network Management System

After you decide which problems require management and determine how you will collect data on the state of the network, your next step is to implement the necessary fault management tools. The tool's effectiveness will rely heavily on the type of information the hosts and devices provide.

A SIMPLE TOOL

The simplest tool would point out the existence of a problem but not indicate its cause. For example, a simple tool could send ICMP Echo messages to each host and device on the data network to test the connectivity up to the IP network layer. If the network were not using TCP/IP, this same test could be performed by having a program repeatedly attempt to connect to each host or device. On a X.25 network, this test could consist of attempting to set up a virtual circuit to each X.121 address within the network. The tool would flag any failures to connect and indicate that further investigation was warranted. Such a tool would be particularly useful if the hosts or devices on the network were not sophisticated enough to send network events.

A MORE COMPLEX TOOL

If hosts and other devices on the network were sufficiently sophisticated to report network events, a more complex tool could be developed to take advantage of this capability. This tool would inform you when it detected a problem by logging network events or by polling. Finding a fault via a critical network event also would help isolate its cause. Flowchart 2.1 shows how this application could work.

To further illustrate how such a tool might work, consider the network management system shown in Fig. 2.3. A T-1 device in this system provides a circuit of 56 kilobits per second (kbps) between two TCP/IP bridge/router (brouter) devices.

The T-1 device performs perfectly, but suppose the circuit provided by the local phone company failed due to a hardware failure. In this case, each brouter

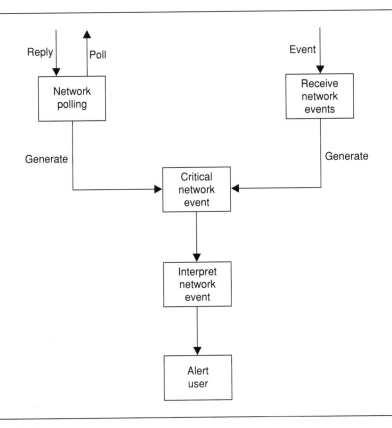

FLOWCHART 2.1
Flowchart of a more complex tool.

would send a critical network event to the network management system. The application would then immediately relay this information to the network engineers.

The DECnet network shown in Fig. 2.4 provides a more complicated example of how the reporting capability of network devices could be used. This network includes a workstation named *Sergeant* that is a DECnet router with one megabyte of memory available for all networking processes and their buffer storage. Unknown to you, this is insufficient memory to cope with the recent network activity on the system. *Sergeant* has one LAN connection and a serial line to a similar DECnet router named *Pepper,* whose configuration assigns five megabytes of memory for networking. As indicated in the diagram, *Sergeant* resides at a small branch office whereas *Pepper* is a concentrator node at a central location. The only way data from *Sergeant* can reach the rest of the company is through the serial link connecting the two routers. Now, suppose a

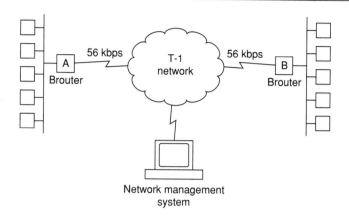

FIGURE 2.3
The T-1 network provides a 56 kbps-circuit between brouter A and brouter B.

sudden burst of traffic caused *Sergeant* to overflow its memory allocated for networking. This would result in a software error that would stop the DECnet routing process, which in turn would cause the system to crash. After a while, *Pepper* would recognize the link had failed and would send a critical network event about the serial link failure to a central fault management tool. It now would be up to the tool to determine if the physical link has indeed failed.

The fault management tool would query *Pepper,* which had just sent the **link down** message. It may then determine whether the serial interface still could hear a *carrier signal,* a continuous wave that is modulated with information on a serial connection. The carrier signal tells a device that the link is operational. If the tool were to report that *Pepper* had sent a **link down** message and that the carrier signal still existed on the link, it could then logically assume that the true cause of the fault might be the failure of *Sergeant.*

However, serial links do fail even though both sides of the connection receive a carrier signal. The link drivers or modems used may send a continuous carrier signal to the brouter whether the actual link is operational or not. To further isolate the fault, the fault management tool could test the link by putting the serial interface on *Pepper* in loopback and instructing the router to test its own interface. Doing this would test the hardware and connectivity on a portion of the link. If this test failed, then the tool should report that although a carrier signal existed on the link in question, data did not traverse this link while in loopback. Additionally, if the link level hardware that supported the link was accessible (a channel bank, DSU/CSU, T-1 multiplexer), the fault management tool could run some physical level tests on the hardware to confirm its operation. Flowchart 2.2 shows how this application could function.

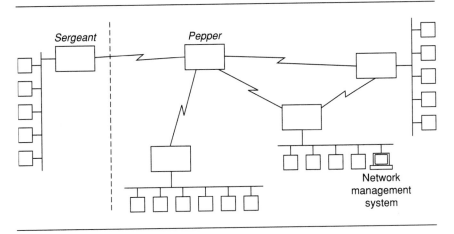

FIGURE 2.4
The DECnet network with *Sergeant* and *Pepper*.

The network management application could now conclude that the fault was caused by either a failure on *Sergeant* or a failure on the link between *Sergeant* and *Pepper*. Considering the information supplied, this would be a reasonable conclusion. Still, you would have no idea what caused *Sergeant* to fail. So after resetting *Sergeant* to clear the problem, most likely the scenario would reoccur during subsequent heavy memory utilizations on the DECnet router. Perhaps only after repeated router failures would it occur to you to examine the configuration of the memory assigned to networking and then to reconfigure *Sergeant* properly.

Reoccurrence of the fault might have been prevented at the time of the first event if *Sergeant* had sent a critical network event message to a fault management tool reporting that it was utilizing 80 percent of its networking memory. Possibly, however, this type of event would not have generated an error message for you. But when the application concluded that the problem resided in the failure of *Sergeant,* it then could have scanned all recent events for any messages sent about that particular router. The additional information could have expedited the fault management process.

AN ADVANCED TOOL

The complex tool just described performs quite a bit of fault management, but it doesn't perform the final step: correcting the problem. In the following example, we see how a fault management tool can resolve the lack of communication between two hosts.

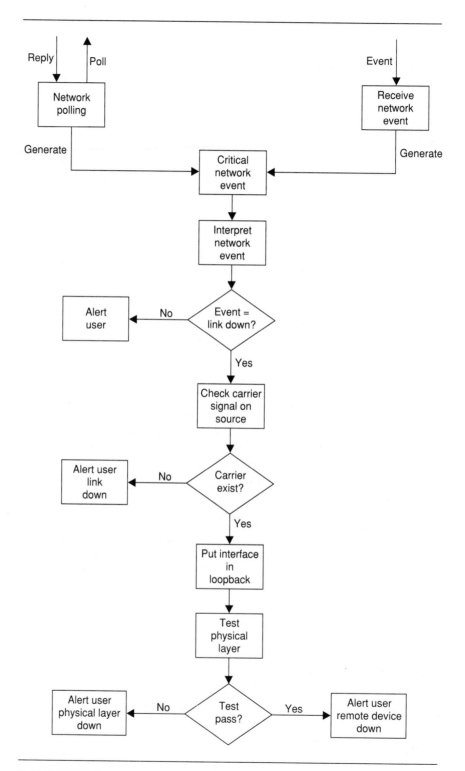

FLOWCHART 2.2

Many faults on a data network result from the failure of a network device, yet the problem does not always lie within the networking hardware. Consider a situation in which two systems cannot communicate across a network. Suppose, for example, a user on *Hermes,* the source system, repeatedly is unsuccessful in its attempts to send an electronic mail message to the destination system, *Zeus* (see Fig. 2.5). Although the fault management tool shows every piece of networking equipment to be operational and no devices have sent any critical events to the tool, it is apparent that part of the network is malfunctioning.

To solve a network problem, it's prudent that we separate the task into smaller, distinct units. In the situation just described, a reasonable approach would be first to determine which devices were providing the current connection between *Hermes* and *Zeus.* Next, you would examine each step along the path, starting at the source. If at any step an error was found, you would examine that piece more closely until the problem was found. Let's look at this strategy in more detail.

The advanced tool would use a network management protocol to look at each device along the path, all the way up to the last device before *Zeus.* (We'll assume both machines can communicate with each device on the path between them but not with each other.) The tool discovers no faults on any of these devices, yet the user still cannot send electronic mail through the network. At this point, the tool would run a new set of tests on each device between the two machines that although time consuming, would check for many possible problems.

One such test could check the error rates on each intermediary system and network device. Doing this may include sending data packets of various sizes

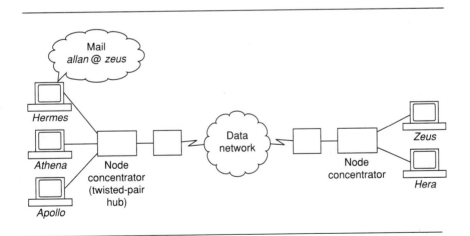

FIGURE 2.5
Hermes cannot send electronic mail to *Zeus.*

from the source to the destination to see if an error occurred. If this test proved inconclusive, the tool then could check the electronic mail process on both systems by attempting to send a message from *Hermes* to *Zeus* and then checking error logs. Or, the tool could try another network service to verify connectivity, such as file transfer, between the two machines.

Hermes attaches to the network via a twisted-pair hub. Using these additional tests, the tool discovers that large data packets that traverse this hub fail over 55 percent of the time. The electronic mail message the user was trying to send was quite large, and the application that broke this message into packets used a large packet size. Thus the tool has isolated the source of the problem.

Determining that the port on the hub could be the problem, the tool could move the port that attaches *Hermes* to the data network (if the software in the hub allows this action). Then, the tool would rerun the test with large data packets. This time, the connection from the hub to *Hermes* transmits 100 percent of the data without an error. The tool has corrected the problem. As a last step, the tool could produce a log of the procedure it used to find the problem so that you could fix the malfunctioning port.

2.4 Impact of a Fault on the Network

A fault management tool must be capable of analyzing how a fault can affect other areas of the data network. Only then could it provide you with a complete fault analysis.

To illustrate this point, consider a common situation in which a satellite connects an organization's DECnet and IBM SNA networks between Europe and the continental United States. If this link failed, the tool would inform you of the failure. The tool would even attempt to fix the problem and then may report it to you in a statement such as the following:

```
LINK FAILURE between Europe Node and United States Node
```

This information would be useful but wouldn't tell you that the failure is cutting off communication between Europe and the United States for DECnet and IBM SNA. With this additional information, however, you would know that the fault required immediate attention. Therefore an alternate version of the preceding statement could read like this:

```
LINK FAILURE between Europe Node and United States Node.
STOPS DECnet and IBM SNA traffic between Europe and United
States.
```

But now let's say the data network for the organization also has a terrestrial link between the continental United States and Europe in addition to the satellite link, with both links servicing DECnet and IBM SNA traffic. Now, when the fault management tool finds the satellite link down, the message might take this form:

```
LINK FAILURE between Europe Node and United States Node.
Impacts DECnet and IBM SNA traffic between Europe and
United States.
```

In this case, traffic would be impacted, but not completely stopped.

In another example, suppose a company has a substantial X.25 network with a large switch in New York that connects Boston, Buffalo, Newark, and Washington DC to the rest of the network (see Fig. 2.6). If at some point the X.25 switch failed, the fault management tool could produce a message such as:

```
SWITCH FAILURE in New York. NO ACCESS to Boston, Buffalo,
Newark, and Washington DC.
```

Thus you would know not only that there had been a failure but also how that failure affected network communication.

Designing a fault management tool that has the capability to report these types of faults and their implications is not very difficult. As we see in the discussion of performance management in Chapter 6, information concerning the type of data traversing a network device can be stored by the network management system for use by fault management tools.

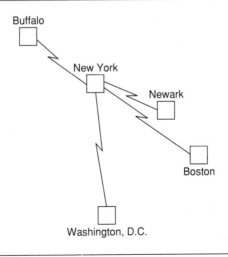

FIGURE 2.6
The X.25 network topology.

2.5 Form of Reporting Faults

The form in which a fault is reported is nearly as important as the fault management process itself. The most common forms messages may take are

- text,
- graphical, and
- auditory signals.

Text messages are an appealing choice because they work on any type of terminal. However, a picture message is most effective. Note that to deliver this type of message, the fault management tool needs access to a color display capable of sophisticated graphics. As the tool ideally will reside on the network management system, this would probably not be a problem. Even without color, one method to catch the engineer's attention is to flash the picture of the device with the fault. An audible bell or noise has an advantage in that it will quickly call an engineer's attention to the tool if the engineer is working in another area. This method may be inadequate, however, if the tool is in a busy operations center with many people and monitoring systems. A combination of message forms may be best. For example, in the case of the failure of the X.25 switch (see Section 2.4), a picture of the fault could have shown New York as a failure site and the outlying sites as those affected. To clarify this graphical display, a text message could have been added.

ADVANTAGE OF COLOR GRAPHICS

While other applications on the network management system may not require color graphics for their outputs, these graphics are particularly useful in fault management. For example, a display of mean time between failure for devices does not depend on the use of color; a text report would probably suffice for this network analysis application. Similarly, in accounting management and security management, simple text displays usually are sufficient to report results.

However, graphics, even without color, will help indicate the status of a network device. Add color and the application can convey network status to you even more efficiently. To see how this might work, consider the following example. A graphical interface could show every device on a map drawn by the network management system. More complex networks might require a hierarchical map, with each node representing a building, a city, or even many cities. Each of these nodes could open into another map, with a finer granularity of nodes (see Fig. 2.7).

Finally, perhaps through many steps, each specific device on the network could be shown. To indicate the status of each device, a color scheme such as

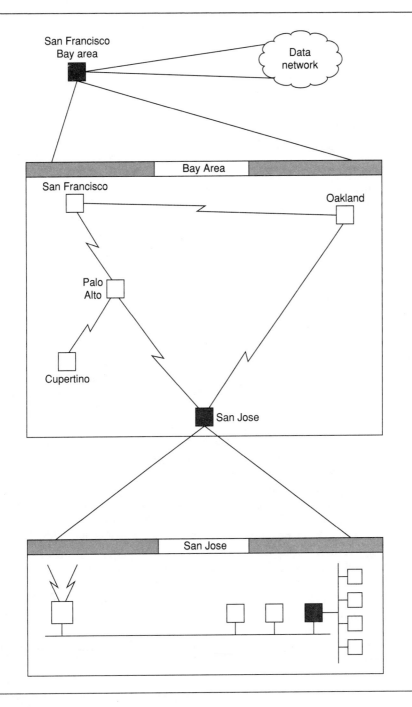

FIGURE 2.7
A hierarchical map was used to isolate a fault.

the following could be used:

- ▪ = green=green device up with no errors
- ▪ = yellow=yellow device may have an error
- ▪ = red=red device in error state
- ▪ = blue=blue device up, but was in error state
- ▪ = orange=orange device misconfigured
- ▪ = gray=gray no information on the device
- ▪ = purple=purple device being polled

According to this scheme, a green device would be one that had not experienced any critical network events and a red device would be one known to have a fault. A red device may be one that no longer answers polls because it does not hear them or it sends unintelligible replies. You could use yellow for those devices that did not respond to *a single poll sequence*—indicating that the device may have an error. In this case, the fault management tool might show a device in a yellow status color until *two* poll intervals occurred without the device responding. Under this condition, you would know that when a device turned yellow, you should wait to see if a *second* poll interval occurred and failed, which would change the device to red and thus signal a situation needing your attention. Otherwise, if a device moved from green to red every time a single poll was lost or not answered, you might see devices go up and down frequently.

If a device was in an error state and then returned to normal operation, the device would change to blue, thus informing you that the device was now up, but that it had recently experienced a fault.

A device that was orange, indicating it was misconfigured, could result from its having an incorrect password, network address, number of interfaces, or the like; you would know to check the configuration of orange devices. If no information could be found about a device, it would be colored gray, indicating it could not be polled or never answered a poll. And finally, purple devices would be those currently being polled so the network engineer could see the progress of the tool.

Whether or not events that affect the devices would also change the color of the nodes higher in the network's hierarchical map would be determined by the network management system. However, in practical use, the layer immediately above the one displayed would change accordingly in response to critical network events.

To see how a hierarchical map might work with the color assignments, picture the entire data network as a cloud. A green cloud would tell the network engineer that no critical events had occurred within the network. If this cloud turned red, the network engineer would know to inspect the graphic interface hierarchy to find a faulty device. Perhaps the cloud may explode into a map of the world on which one particular city was colored red. The network topology of the city could then be accessed with the faulty device shown in red. A report then could detail for the engineer the steps the system already had taken to correct the fault.

Summary

A network engineer who uses a fault management tool on a data network will be able to take advantage of increased personal efficiency as well as greater network efficiency and reliability.

Fault management involves three major aspects. First, the fault must be identified. Next, the cause of the fault must be isolated. Finally, the fault must be corrected.

The first step in the process—identifying the fault—includes determining how best to gather information about the network. We can use one or preferably both of the following methods: logging critical network events or occasionally polling network devices.

Also included in the information gathering process is determination of which faults to manage for a particular data network. Network engineers should be guided in this determination by the following factors:

1. The scope of control over the network, which affects the amount of information obtainable from network devices

2. The size of the network

We also discussed a variety of tools, from simple to advanced, designed to facilitate fault management. The simple tool would merely point out the existence of a fault but not tell us its cause. A more complex tool would take advantage of the capability of hosts and devices to send critical network events, which would facilitate isolating the cause of the fault. The advanced tool would go one step further by correcting the fault.

We also stressed the impact a fault can have on other parts of the network and set out the methods of reporting faults, with particular emphasis on using color graphics to relay fault messages.

For Further Study

Bosack, L. and Hedrick, C. *Problems in Large LANs,* IEEE Network Magazine, Volume 2, January 1988.

Dauber, S., *Finding Fault,* Byte Magazine, March 1991.

3

Configuration Management

In this chapter:
- Definition of configuration management
- Benefits of the configuration management process
- Methods of obtaining configuration data
- Ways of storing configuration information
- Examples of possible configuration management tools
- Flowcharts of configuration management tools
- Types of configuration reports

Configuration management is the process of obtaining data from the network and using that data to manage the setup of all network devices. It consists of

- gathering information about the current network configuration,
- using that data to modify the network configuration of the network devices, and
- storing the data, maintaining an up-to-date inventory, and producing reports based on the data.

In this chapter, we present the benefits of configuration management to the network engineer and discuss further the three steps involved in this form of management. We then present three levels of configuration management tools for you to consider and review the various reports that can be obtained from configuration data.

3.1 Benefits of the Configuration Management Process

The primary benefit of configuration management is that it enhances the network engineer's control over the configuration of network devices. It does this by offering rapid access to vital configuration data regarding those devices.

37

On more complex systems, it also can enable the engineer to compare the running configuration with that stored in the system and to change the configurations easily as needed.

For example, configuration data usually includes the current setup of each network device, information that is invaluable to the engineer. Let's suppose you are considering additional interfaces for a particular device. You would want to know first the number of physical interfaces already in the device. You also would want to know the network addresses assigned to the interfaces, for this data would help you configure the software on the device. With configuration management in place, you could locate this information easily.

In some cases, a device may need to be modified. For example, consider an interface on a device that is causing errors on a LAN segment. Using a configuration management tool, you could remotely reconfigure the device to deactivate this interface. Let's say you then examine the interface's configuration and notice that an incorrect software parameter is causing the errors. The configuration management tool could enable you to change the incorrect parameter to the proper setting and then reactivate the interface.

Configuration management can help a network engineer further by providing an up-to-date inventory of network components. There are many applications for this inventory; for example, it can enable you to determine how many of a specific type of device currently exist on the network. The inventory also could aid in producing a report on all versions of an operating system that are currently in use (see Fig. 3.1) on devices throughout the network.

The inventory facility of configuration management need not be limited to tracking network devices. You could use it to record, among other things, vendor contact information, leased line circuit numbers, or the quantity of network spares. In this regard, the practicality of a comprehensive inventory cannot be overemphasized. For example, armed with data about the number of units purchased from a vendor, you may be in a position to negotiate volume discounts from that vendor. Or if data shows that a leased line is operational only 50 percent of a given time period, by using the inventory data you can check the number of circuits purchased from the same vendor. With this information you can press for better customer service.

NOTE: Network inventory data should be considered confidential. In the hands of a malicious person, this data could harm the network in many ways. For example, someone learns about a bug in the software of a certain device that can render the device inoperable. By getting the network inventory list and finding out how many of those devices are in the network, he could cause a massive network failure by triggering the bug on all devices. We discuss security management and guarding the confidentiality of information in Chapter 4.

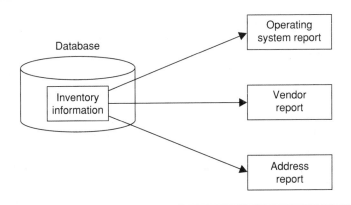

FIGURE 3.1
Network inventory data can be used to produce reports for network engineers.

3.2 Accomplishing Configuration Management

Configuration management consists of the following steps:

1. Gather information about the current network environment

   Failure to perform this step can result in the network engineer's wasting time on network problems caused by simple configuration errors. Collecting this data can be done manually by the engineer or automatically by the system.

2. Use that data to modify the configuration of the network device

   A data network environment is continuously changing. The ability to modify its current configuration in real-time is essential. Modification would probably be manual if the data collection method were manual, automatic if the collection method were automatic.

3. Store the data, maintain an up-to-date inventory of all network components, and produce various reports

We discuss each of these steps next.

COLLECTING DATA MANUALLY

Obtaining information from the network often begins with a manual effort. You may have to use remote login to reach each device on the network and then record the device's serial number in a notebook and its address assignments in a spreadsheet or flat ASCII file. While a manual effort will produce the desired result, using it to keep records up-to-date in an ever-changing data network environment can be difficult, time consuming, and monotonous.

For example, suppose you need to track in a table every network address assigned to a 5000-node network. This information may be sorted to facilitate easy address retrieval. With the addition of each new piece of equipment, you would have to acquire the pertinent data and then enter and re-sort it, obviously a tedious process when done manually.

Further, manual tracking of configurations works well only if you can find all the network devices. New systems added to the network by a user unbeknownst to you can be difficult to detect. Even for those new systems you know about, obtaining the configuration information may involve your traveling to the site of the system or enlisting the aid of someone locally to gather the data.

COLLECTING DATA AUTOMATICALLY

The laborious task of manually acquiring and updating configuration data can be avoided when you use automatic methods. For example, you could employ a network management protocol to obtain data about network devices regularly and to record that data automatically in the storage facility.

Another tool you can use is auto-discovery, which can produce a current listing of all devices on the network. Auto-discovery also can help produce a graphical map of the current data network using a process called auto-mapping as seen in Fig. 3.2. Although you may need to modify a map produced by

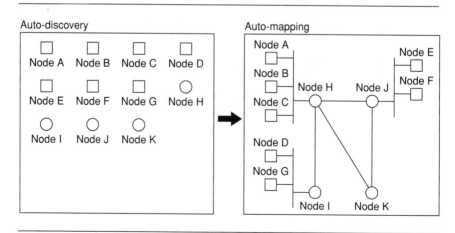

FIGURE 3.2
Auto-discovery discovers devices on the network while auto-mapping produces useful configuration information in the form of a network map.

auto-mapping before it fully reflects the geographic or functional layout of the network, once these changes are made the map is useful for showing the overall network configuration.

The amount of bandwidth an automatic configuration process consumes will of course will influence your decision to use the method, although the benefits of automation should easily justify the costs. As in the case of fault management, the frequency at which network devices are polled will affect the amount of bandwidth consumption. Accordingly, you would want to determine the appropriate frequency with which to gather this information; because network configurations usually change relatively infrequently, this polling may be as often as only once a week, thus keeping the amount of bandwidth consumption low.

MODIFYING CONFIGURATION DATA

Once configuration management information has been obtained, it will usually need to be updated. Consider again the 5000-node network discussed in the section on manual data collection. If only 1 percent of these machines required an address assignment or change every week, you still would have to track 50 modifications a week. Moreover, network addresses are but one of many pieces of configuration management data. For any single device, there could be dozens of modifiable parameters to be tracked.

Obviously, a manual method would be inefficient for this data process. Also, unless the engineer who did the manual configuration recorded her steps, a record of configuration changes would not be kept. This could lead to confusion when another network engineer examines the configuration of the changed device. In contrast, if the configuration management process allows the changing of the device configurations on the network management system, these changes could be recorded before they were sent to the device. As an added advantage, the network management system might be able to verify that the configuration changes are appropriate to the device and warn the engineer before she inadvertently misconfigured the device.

STORING INFORMATION

Configuration management also should provide a means for information storage. An efficient management system would store the entire configuration of a data network in a central location, thus placing configuration data within quick and efficient access by the network engineer. This single location could be a notebook or a PC-based spreadsheet in a network control center, as shown in Fig. 3.2. Regardless of which method is used, the consistency and availability of data is invaluable to the network engineer.

One common storage medium to use on a computer is the ASCII file. This medium has two advantages: ASCII is easy to read and its file structure is usually easy to understand and administer. Because of this, most application programs (regardless of the hardware platform) have the capability of reading ASCII files. However, it also has significant disadvantages. ASCII characters use considerable storage space in a computer system; vast amounts of data stored in this manner can consume valuable disk space. Further, the uncomplicated structure of ASCII files, while an advantage in some respects, in this case makes for slow access during search procedures. But perhaps an even more important disadvantage is that ASCII files are unable to provide complex relationships between data.

This latter deficiency of ASCII files leads one to the more efficient alternative: a *relational database management system,* or RDBMS. An RDBMS offers many advantages over ASCII files for data storage:

- It stores data efficiently, enabling large amounts to reside on a single computer.
- It stores data in its own format, which allows for fast searching for specific data.
- It can automatically sort stored data in various ways.
- It usually can automatically restore lost data.
- It enables the user to relate various types of data to one another.

Although the first four benefits listed may seem to comprise sufficient argument for using an RDBMS, perhaps its main advantage is the fifth one— enabling the user to relate various types of information to one another. Figure 3.3 shows, for example, that configuration data for a particular device may direct the engineer to the device's vendor. This vendor data may in turn point to a specific person in the vendor organization to contact if a problem occurs on the device.

The flow of related information is not restricted to network devices; it can include all information necessary for configuration management. Thus using an RDBMS for storage can help the network engineer in all aspects of the configuration management process.

Note, however, an RDBMS does have disadvantages: (1) It often involves a complex set of intricate administration procedures; (2) it uses its own language, which the engineer may not know; and (3) since an RDBMS is much more complex, it is often tied to a particular operating system or hardware platform. This makes the data stored in the RDBMS difficult to move from one system to another. Most RDBMS vendors have solved the latter disadvantage by allowing data in the RDBMS to be put into ASCII format—gaining the ease of transportability and use. The benefits an RDBMS can provide, however, may very well offset its disadvantages. We discuss these factors in the next section when we introduce you to an advanced tool for configuration management.

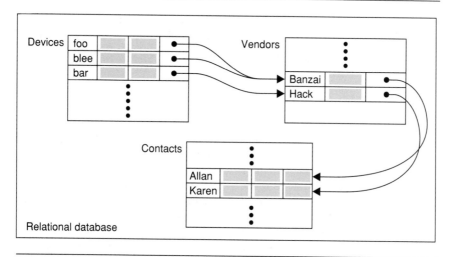

FIGURE 3.3
A RDBMS allows the building of relationships between data.

3.3 Configuration Management on a Network Management System

As we have seen, configuration management tools can increase the network engineer's productivity by

- in some cases, automatically gathering and updating data on network devices,
- providing for central storage of configuration data,
- enabling modification of network data, and
- facilitating the production of network inventory and other reports.

Which of these facilities a tool can provide will depend on its complexity, which we will see as we next examine the three levels of configuration management tools available to the engineer.

A SIMPLE TOOL

A simple configuration management tool, at the very least, should fulfill the requirement of providing for central storage of all data network information, such as network address assignments, serial numbers, physical locations, and other pertinent data for devices. However, you still would have to undertake the laborious and time-consuming task of manually entering all the required data into the tool. A simple tool also could provide another important facility, a search function, which would enable you to locate information easily.

A MORE COMPLEX TOOL

A more complex tool could be developed by adding a feature to automatically gather and store information from all network devices. This tool also could be designed to compare a device's current configuration with that stored in the system. It further could enable you to change a device's running configuration. And finally, as with a simple tool, the more complex version should provide for centralized storage and easy retrieval of data (although at this level of complexity, the manner in which the tool stores the data would not be important as long as it provided for easy retrieval). Let's discuss some of these features further.

The automatic data-acquisition feature of a configuration management tool is particularly important because it ensures the information obtained will be current. Thus assured that the data is up-to-date, you probably would feel more confident about polling devices only when necessary or during periods of low network usage. (The frequency of updates would be a configurable parameter.) Ideally, the tool would use a network management protocol to canvass the devices and get their configuration data.

As illustrated in Fig. 3.4, the tool also should enable you to compare a device's running configuration against its stored configuration. Further, it should either initiate a process that would enable you to change the configuration or perform the change itself automatically. In a common scenario, the tool would probe the device for its current setup. Next, it would compare this setup against the stored configuration. If any discrepancies were found, the tool would ask you if it should change the device configuration to match the stored version.

Note that not all configuration details will always equally important. Therefore, to work well in different data network environments, the tool should include the means by which you can specify which configuration errors generate warning messages and which prompt an alarm. For example, on a terminal server, there could be an option to configure the bit rate for an incoming connection, which would be useful for simultaneously communicating with many devices at different bit rates. Suppose that stored configuration information indicated that each asynchronous line out of the terminal server should be set at 9600 bits per second (bps). However, when the tool queried the device, one line was found to be set at 2400 bps. In this instance, the tool may not care about the configuration, but simply would issue a warning message to a log file. In contrast, if the tool found a secure line on the terminal server without a password, it would alert you of the situation by immediately setting off an alarm.

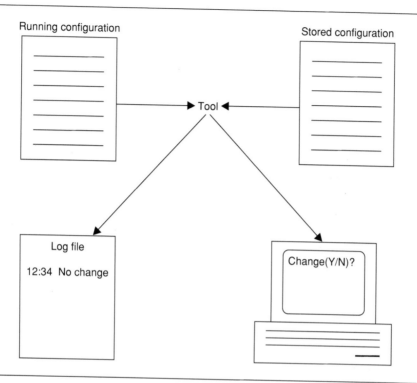

Running configuration

Stored configuration

Tool

Log file

12:34 No change

Change(Y/N)?

FIGURE 3.4
A configuration management tool can compare a device's running configuration with a stored configuration and can note differences between them. It also can prompt the network engineer for input.

Flowchart 3.1 shows how a tool could check the current operating system, IP address, and subnet mask of each device on the network against the stored configuration. In this case, if the version of the operating system for the device does not match the stored configuration, the tool would simply report the difference. However, if the tool found a different IP address or subnet mask, it would report the discrepancy and reset the configuration to match the stored values.

AN ADVANCED TOOL

While the more complex tool would allow for changing the running configuration of a device, an advanced configuration management tool would be even more effective if it used a relational database (RDBMS) to store, relate, query,

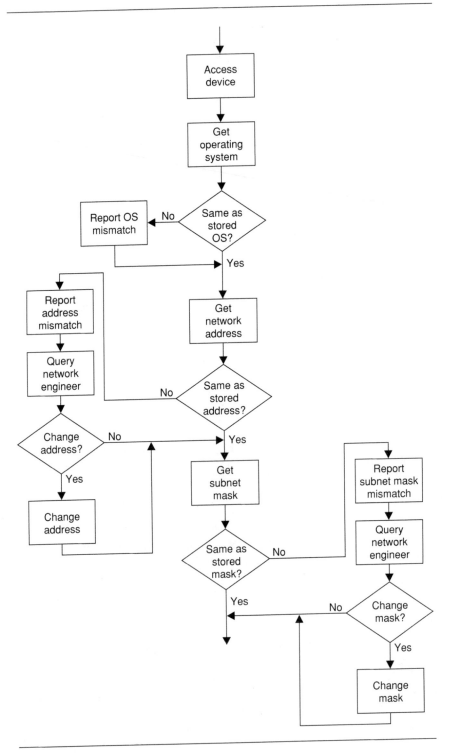

FLOWCHART 3.1
Functionality in the more complex tool.

and inventory network information. To be optimally functional, the tool also would be capable of evaluating device configurations.

A tool's ability to relate one set of data to another is important for configuration management. For example, one engineer may be responsible for over one hundred devices. Obviously, relating this engineer's name to all the devices would be easier than entering and storing the same name once for each device.

An RDBMS not only allows for complex manipulation of data, but also permits complex queries. These queries usually are written in the *Structured Query Language (SQL)*.[1] Using SQL, you can find specific information stored within the database. Suppose, for example, you discover that version A of a software program on an Ethernet bridge is causing network errors. To correct this situation, you first would need to find all bridges running that software version. Let's say that all the possible devices on the network are stored in a table named *devices*. Therefore, to find all affected Ethernet bridges, you could issue the following SQL command:

```
SELECT * FROM devices WHERE type = bridge AND software = A
```

The output resulting from this command would show you all bridge devices in the table *devices* that are running software version A (see Fig. 3.5).

Device name	Vendor	Serial #	Type	Software	Location	Contact
ENGRBR1	RouteMe	0180106	bridge	A	ENGR	Allan
ADMINBR	BridgeIt	AB62	bridge	A	Admin	Boss
MKTGBR23	BridgeIt	AB2301	bridge	A	Bldg10	Karen

FIGURE 3.5
The possible output from a sample SQL query.

[1]SQL is defined by ANSI as a standard language for communicating with relational databases.

SQL queries also can produce output such as *inventory reports*. The inventory should include for a network device its

- serial number,
- make and model,
- operating system,
- RAM capacity,
- network addresses, and
- interface capacity.

Let's say you want to generate a report showing all devices, and their serial numbers, made by a specific vendor that were added to the network within the past year and therefore are still under their one-year warranties. You could use an SQL query such as the following:

```
SELECT device,sn FROM devices,vendors WHERE vendors.name =
Banzai AND devices.months <= 12
```

The resulting report would show all the devices and their serial numbers on the network from the Banzai Company that are still under their one-year warranty (see Fig. 3.6).

Other reports you could generate using an RDBMS are vendor contact inventories and leased circuit inventories. For example, in an inventory of vendor information report, you might want to include the vendor's

- name,
- address,
- maintenance contact/phone number,
- sales contact/phone number, and
- main phone number.

An inventory of leased circuits may include the

- circuit ID,
- speed,
- vendor,
- end points on network, and
- known down times.

While you could compose ad hoc SQL queries to explore specific parts of the database, it really shouldn't be necessary for you to learn SQL. Rather, ideally, the tool should provide an interface to help you locate critical data stored within the database without your having to use SQL. The tool should ask you for the data to search for, then follow all pertinent relationships, and finally,

Device name	Serial #
Perfect	BB00888
Reno	BB1298
Pecos	BB11072
New Jersey	BB572
Blue Blazer	BB11

FIGURE 3.6
The listing of all devices from the Banzai Company on the network still under their one-year warranty.

present the information in a form you can understand. For example, finding a device at address P.Q should not require you to know that the address resides in the database table called *addresses*. Instead, you should be able simply to tell the tool to find P.Q and then be shown all known information about the device, including the device's physical location, its administrator, its hardware description, and so forth.

So far we have characterized our advanced tool as one that can store the necessary information, compare it to current configurations, modify those configurations, and handle queries. Now let's consider an additional feature: evaluation. Periodically, the tool should evaluate the configuration of all network devices and show you where duplicate network addresses, names, or functions are employed. Suppose, for example, that a LAN has grown without management. On this LAN exists many PC file servers. The configuration management tool could tell you that two of these servers provide the same information and applications to the users. This may be intentional redundancy, on the other hand, it could be a configuration management issue in need of resolution.

In another example, the tool could evaluate the communication capabilities of the network configuration. WAN devices, such as cluster controllers and front-end processors, require configuration of their interfaces in order to communicate at the proper speed. In a typical setup (see Fig. 3.7), many cluster controllers exist at a single site with WAN links back to the central site, which houses a mainframe computer. Suppose that on one controller, the response

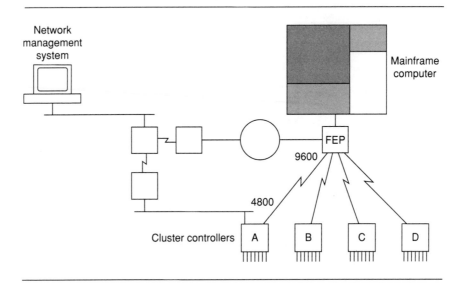

FIGURE 3.7
The setup with a configuration error brought to the attention of the network engineer by the configuration management tool.

time from each terminal was slower than that from terminals on the other controllers. The configuration management tool, upon evaluating this setup, would recognize that the speed setting on that cluster controller was set to transmit at 4800 bps while the front-end processor at the other side of the link was set to receive at a maximum of 9600 bps, resulting in a maximum speed of 4800 bps. In contrast, all the other cluster controllers at the same site and talking to the same front-end processor were set up for 9600 bps communications on both sides. The tool would conclude that the discrepancy in bit rate of the controller in question caused its slower response time. As a final step in the evaluation, the tool would use the relational database to determine the actual speed of the wide area link. Thus, the tool would have found a problem in the network configuration automatically by evaluating the configuration management information.

3.4 Generating Configuration Reports

In the preceding discussion, we emphasized that a configuration management tool must generate reports that enable the engineer to keep abreast of the overall network configuration. Although this type of tool generally is not required to relay information as quickly as is a fault management tool, there are special cases where prompt reporting is necessary, such as when the tool finds duplicate network addresses or names. Also in contrast to fault management, a configuration management tool does not depend on the use of color or a graphical interface to be totally functional. Provided the engineer has access to the data on an ASCII terminal, the full range of configuration management facilities are potentially still available. Of course, the easier the tool makes it for the engineer to generate the necessary reports, the more likely the tool will be used.

One type of report details the overall configuration of each network device, including as applicable its name, network addresses, serial number, manufacturer, operating system, and the local person responsible for it. If the device is attached to serial links, the report also could list circuit numbers, useful for reporting link failures to circuit vendors. Other optional data that could be included are the vendor contact name and the device's physical location. The above information represents the minimum you would probably want for each network device. The frequency with which this report is generated would vary for each network, ranging, for example, from weekly on a rapidly changing network to monthly on a stable network.

Armed with this report on the current network setup, you next would need a summary of all the recent network modifications. This report should list all the changes to the network by category, the names of those who made the changes, and when the changes took place. Categories could include all new devices and changes in hardware, software, and administration. By subcategorizing this report, you can quickly access important information. As with the network configuration report, the frequency with which you have this report generated will vary depending upon how often the network changed.

Finally, the configuration management tool should create a summary report on the total network inventory. This report, crucial for the bookkeeping effort necessary on any data network, would most likely need to focus only on devices. For each piece of equipment purchased, the report should show its serial number, physical location, date put in service, length and type of warranty, and complete upgrade history. Depending on the network environment, additional information on each device may be required. Because it usually is necessary only for bookkeeping purposes, this report could be produced as infrequently as monthly.

Summary

Managing the configuration of a host of network devices in various physical locations is a demanding but necessary task for the network engineer. Its challenge is to provide the engineer with the means to handle the various aspects of this task most efficiently.

Configuration management offers the following benefits:

- In some cases, it automatically gathers and updates data on network devices.
- It provides a central storage location for configuration data. This location could be as simple as a notebook or as complex as a relational database system.
- It enables the network engineer to modify network configuration on line.
- It facilitates the production of network inventory and other reports.

The configuration management process involves three steps: (1) obtaining information from the data network, (2) modifying the configuration of the network devices, and (3) storing the information for future use. These steps may be accomplished in methods ranging from manual data entry and retrieval to automated data entry and retrieval into a sophisticated relational database system.

On a network management system, a configuration management tool can enable the network engineer to accomplish these tasks easily and efficiently. A simple tool can give the engineer a central location for storing information. A more complex tool also can provide a way to automatically obtain information from the network, to compare a device's running configuration against its stored configuration, and to change the configuration automatically. An advanced tool can go a step further by using a relational database to relate one set of data to another, permit queries to the RDBMS, and evaluate the configuration of the entire network.

A final aspect of configuration management involves producing reports pertaining to specific device setups, recent network modifications, and inventory. These reports can be generated automatically or on demand as needed by the network engineer.

For Further Study

Madron T., *Enterprise-Wide Computing,* John Wiley and Sons, Inc., New York, 1991.

Rhodes, P., *Lan Operations,* Addison-Wesley Publishing Company, Reading, Mass., 1991.

4

Security Management

In this chapter:
- Definition of security management
- Benefits of the security management process
- Steps in accomplishing security management
- Security useful when attaching to a public data network
- Examples of possible security management tools
- Reporting of security events

Security management involves protecting sensitive information found on devices attached to a data network by controlling access points to that information. *Sensitive information* is any data an organization wants to secure, such as that pertaining to payroll, customer accounts, research and development schedules—the possibilities are limitless.

Security management enables network engineers to protect sensitive information by

- limiting the access to hosts and network devices by users (both inside and outside of the organization) and
- notifying the engineer of attempted or actual breaches of security.

It consists of

- identifying the sensitive information to be protected,
- finding the access points,
- securing the access points, and
- maintaining the secure access points.

This form of security management should not be confused with operating system security or physical security. Protection via security management is achieved through specific configuration of network hosts and devices to control access points within the data network. Access points may include software services, hardware components, and network media. On the other hand, operating system security involves setting up file, directory, and/or program protection, while physical security involves locking computer room doors, installing card access systems, and/or providing for locks on keyboards. However, although these latter two security systems are not a part of security management, without them security management would be useless. Properly set up and administered, security management can prevent an unauthorized person from accessing hosts via a data network; however, if the same person can walk up to the computer and remove the disk drive containing the sensitive information, the data is not secure.

In this chapter, we present the benefits of security management and follow with a discussion of the four steps required to accomplish it. Then we offer you three security management tools, from simple to advanced, for your consideration. Last, we discuss the advantages of an audit trail, which can be obtained from reports of security events. We strongly urge you to read this chapter and then research this topic further in relation to the specific needs of your data network.

4.1 Benefits of the Security Management Process

The primary concern many users have about attaching hosts to a data network is the potential lack of security for sensitive information located on the host. To avoid this problem, a host possessing sensitive information could eliminate network access altogether and transfer information via movable media (i.e. magnetic tape, optical discs and so forth). In this way, only those people with the physical security access to the host could reach the sensitive information. However, this method, although secure, is not particularly efficient.

Properly set up and maintained security management can offer a more practical alternative while assuaging users' security concerns and increasing their confidence in the network's effectiveness and security. This building of confidence and the actual securing of sensitive information are the main benefits of security management.

The drawbacks of not having security management on a network are easy to envision. Suppose an organization's private data network connects to a public data network and suppose further that a computer within the company network that contains payroll information also provides a service that gives any user any information requested. As you can see, the consequences of such unrestricted access could be catastrophic for the organization.

The disastrous results a lack of security management can produce was dramatically demonstrated in November 1988, when the *Internet Worm* was let loose. Using services that were inadequately secured to gain access to information on hosts throughout the Internet, this worm proceeded to propagate throughout hundreds of computer networks. One method the worm used was a

UNIX service called *sendmail* to connect to a computer, spawn a shell, and then execute itself. Some versions of *sendmail* even allowed the worm access to one of the program's debugging modes without imposing any security. The worm also used another UNIX service called *finger* to gain privileges on hosts. The *sendmail* and *finger* attacks are examples of the worm exploiting security weaknesses in a network access point. Interestingly, the most successful method the worm used to log in to hosts was simply to try common passwords, a host security weakness. The worm could have destroyed file systems, corrupted data, or performed many other malicious actions. Fortunately, it was not written with this intent; however, because it reproduced itself many times, the worm brought numerous computers to a halt because of excessive processor load.

Another vivid example of how inadequate security management can hurt an organization is given in the book, *The Cuckoo's Egg,* by Clifford Stoll. This book relates how the author watched as a devious user walked easily through some well-known access points on a data network, none of which were secured.

4.2 Accomplishing Security Management

Effecting security management requires the network engineer to balance the need to secure sensitive information with the needs of users to access information pertinent to performing their jobs. This form of network management involves the following four steps:

1. Identify the sensitive information.
2. Find the access points.
3. Secure the access points.
4. Maintain the secure access points.

These points are illustrated in Fig. 4.1.

First, let's view these steps in a common everyday example. Suppose you recently bought a house and have decided to secure the contents of the house. Instead of putting locks on each item, you might instead *find the access points* by determining that it is the windows and exterior doors of the house that require securing. Accordingly, you would then *secure the access points* by installing locks on each such door and window. Further, to ensure that not just anyone can unlock the doors, you would have only one copy of the keys made for your own use. At this point, you feel confident that the access points—the windows and exterior doors—are secure.

However, just because all the windows and exterior doors are locked does not mean your possessions are fully secured. Someone could easily enter the

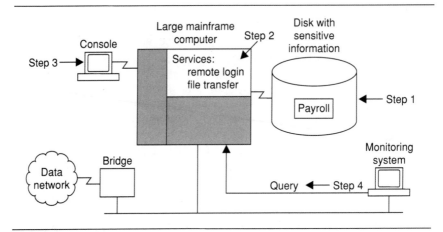

FIGURE 4.1
The four steps involved with security management are: identify the sensitive information (Step 1), find the access points (Step 2), secure the access points (Step 3) and maintain the secure access points (Step 4). Here, the payroll data on the large mainframe is sensitive information. The access points are remote login and file transfer. The engineer secures the access points by configuring the system on the console to only permit authorized users. The monitoring system ensures the maintenance of the security by logging unauthorized login attempts.

house either through a door left unlocked or by breaking and climbing in a window. Therefore you would want to *maintain* the house's access points by checking periodically for unlocked doors and broken windows.

Next, let's consider an example related to data networks. A computer that stores a company's payroll data, which has been defined by the organization as sensitive information, has only one access point: through the data network, using a remote login program. You therefore would need to control this remote login program. To do this, you first could ensure that only people possessing proper authorization to see the payroll information would have user accounts. Next, you could ensure the login program required passwords for each user account. To enhance security further, you also could have the password program give out randomly generated passwords that require periodic renewal. Thus having installed these security measures, you might feel confident that you have secured the sensitive information.

Yet, this single perimeter of defense may not be enough. In addition to requiring passwords for each account, you might want to provide that remote login requests to the payroll host may come only from *authorized remote hosts*. Therefore, to gain access to the payroll data, a user would have to first log on to an authorized remote host and authenticate himself with a password. Then the user could proceed to log on to the payroll machine—again going through a user and password authentication sequence.

Note that in the above examples, we did not attempt to secure the sensitive information itself. In the first example, the solution was not to put all your possessions in a safe. Similarly, in the second instance, we didn't concern ourselves with the physical security of the payroll computer or its file protection scheme, which are not part of network security management.

Also, be aware that in some cases, not every point of access will require securing. For example, suppose a payroll computer accessible via remote login also provides a service to tell network users the time, which usually is not sensitive information. In this case, you would want to allow free access to the time service but limit access to the payroll information (see Fig. 4.2).

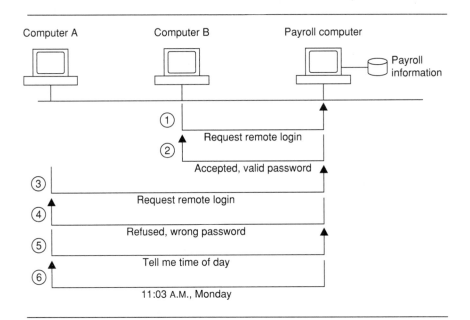

FIGURE 4.2
A user on Computer B makes a remote login request to the payroll computer (1) and is accepted because the user enters a valid password (2). A user on Computer A tries to login remotely to the payroll computer (3) and is denied because the password was wrong (4). Yet, the same user can ask the payroll computer for the time of day (5) and get a response (6). Payroll information is sensitive while the time of day is not.

In the next several sections, we explore in detail the four steps of security management.

IDENTIFYING SENSITIVE INFORMATION

Your first step in accomplishing security management is to determine which hosts on the network have sensitive information. Most organizations have well-defined policies regarding what information qualifies as sensitive; often it includes accounting, financial, customer, market, engineering, and employee information. So at first glance, this process may seem straightforward. However, what is defined as sensitive can differ depending on the environment, for each such environment potentially can have sensitive information unique to it. Further, the most difficult part of identifying sensitive information can be finding on which hosts the data resides.

FINDING THE ACCESS POINTS

Once you know what information is sensitive and where it is located, you next would want to find out how network users can access it. This often tedious process will usually require you to examine each piece of software offering a service via the network—and many computers may have dozens of such programs. The access these programs have to the data network constitute the access points to the sensitive information on the computer, as illustrated in Fig. 4.3. Fortunately, on some computers you can simplify the task of locating access points by isolating how the computer provides for remote login and file transfer.

Most computers on a data network provide for remote login by users. If this login facility doesn't identify users uniquely and limit their movements within the system only to authorized areas, you would want to examine this access point as possibly needing to be secured.

Also, many computers can perform file transfers across the data network. Like the remote login facility, if this service cannot uniquely identify users, its use should be limited. An example of a file transfer service that would require security management scrutiny is the 'anonymous' login in FTP. FTP is the file transfer protocol used by many TCP/IP hosts and many versions of it allow users to login with the user name 'anonymous'. The password for this account is not used, so users can type any string for the password and be logged into a special account in the remote system. The saving grace of this 'anonymous' login is that the files the user can retrieve from this account usually are limited to a small subset of directories. This configuration of FTP often is used to distribute public software and documents. This application also can be used when the computer administrator doesn't care who can access the files in the

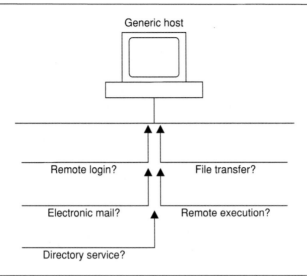

FIGURE 4.3
Identify the access points for each computer.

limited directory structure. Thus, if a computer offers the 'anonymous' login to the FTP service, network engineers for that computer must carefully regulate what information is contained in the accessible directories.

Remote login and file transfer are probably the most popular types of software that provide access points into a computer. However, other programs, such as electronic mail, remote process execution, file and directory servers, and name servers also may give access points into a computer that need to be secured using security management. For example, on a computer running UNIX the services offered by the computer appear in the file */etc/services,* which maps application names to service ports for use by a network transport protocol. Similarly, many personal computers have a file or application that lists the services the computer can offer.

Many computers offer seemingly nonsensitive information through network management protocols. However, on closer examination of the information you may discover that restricted access should be enforced. For example, nearly every network management protocol has the ability to ask a computer for basic information, such as network addresses, names, operating system versions, and length of time in operation—generally innocuous information. Suppose, however, that the computer running the network management protocol is testing a new version of the operating system for the vendor. When queried by a competitor, the operating system version returned is one not yet publicly known. This leak of information, although small, may affect the marketing of competitors' products.

Facilities which allow users to monitor packets as they traverse network media are another access point to sensitive information. Sometimes, the need to gather packets is required to examine why the network is functioning in a certain manner. This is often done with a protocol analyzer or host. The need for this functionality often outweighs any security concerns, because if the network does not function properly no sensitive data will traverse it. However, network engineers should be aware that users do have this ability and can gather packets and potentially discover passwords or other sensitive information.

Another often overlooked location which contains sensitive information on the data network is the network management system itself. The network management system gives the users many methods for discovering sensitive information, both on the network itself and from within the relational database. When determining the access points to a data network, you should consider the network management system as a host that needs special security considerations. The methods used to secure a host are described in the next section.

Many organizations commit substantial resources to standardize security points for all their network devices and hosts. These network security standards serve as a rule for dealing with the many ways to access sensitive information. You can establish these standards along any number of parameters; for example, you could define access points by host manufacturer or type of operating system. In these cases, the organization could decide that all hosts from a certain manufacturer with sensitive information cannot have an 'anonymous' login for FTP, or it could determine that a network software package for personal computers does not provide enough security and so prohibit its use.

SECURING THE ACCESS POINTS

The next step in security management is to apply the necessary security techniques. Security can be employed at multiple layers on the data network:

- On the data link level, you could use encryption.
- Network devices may secure traffic flow based upon packet filters.
- On every host, each access point to information could have an associated service and each of those services that gives access to sensitive information could provide one or more of three different types of security: host authentication, user authentication, and key authentication.

Encryption.   Encryption of data as it traverses a LAN or WAN can prevent unauthorized access to sensitive information. *Encryption* means to encode, and in this case, an encryption device uses an algorithm to scramble, or encode, information to be sent. After the information is relayed, it is unscrambled at the receiving end by performing the reverse of the algorithm to get back to the original information. The algorithm relies on encryption keys that ensure both the sender and receiver are encrypting and de-encrypting data the same way. This key is either software or hardware for each device performing encryption. Encryption is very useful when sending data over satellite and microwave links, which involve transmitting information through the air where it is susceptible to being received by anyone, authorized or not, who can receive the signal.

Encryption's main benefit is that only authorized people—that is, those who have access to the encryption key—can access the sensitive data. But the method is not foolproof. Anyone who studies encrypted data long enough may be able to break even the most complicated key. For example, even the Data Encryption Standard (DES) used by many organizations and devices has a remote chance of being broken.[1]

Because of this possibility of a key being broken, you would want to change keys on a regular basis. Doing this would involve the physical transfer of a new key (either software or hardware) to each device performing encryption. The physical transfer of keys can be time and resource consuming, but it is the safest method for transferring keys (if the key were sent electronically, and the old key had been broken, the new key would be compromised). Although encryption devices can be difficult to maintain, many organizations prefer to use this method for securing sensitive information.

Packet Filtering.   Many network devices, such as routers and bridges, can perform packet filtering based upon network or MAC (media access control) addresses. *Packet filtering* stops packets to or from unsecured hosts before they reach an access point that may yield sensitive information. However, although this approach may help provide security, it does present problems.

First is the need to configure the packet filters within each network device. This means that for each new address or change in address, you would need to change the filters. Second, using a filter doesn't work if the unsecured host changes addresses without telling you. For example, consider an Ethernet bridge that filters packets between segments based on a MAC address. Now, MAC addresses typically are burned into a read-only memory (ROM) chip on the Ethernet interface. Therefore, if the interface board on the unsecured host were to be changed, the new board will not contain the same only MAC address. This would result in the packet filters no longer stopping information to and from the unsecured host. This problem could be caused not only by devious users, but also by a network engineer who changes the interface because it is

---

[1]The chances of breaking a DES key is near 1×10^{72}.

defective or needs upgrading, without realizing that the new board has a new MAC address. Some hosts provide software configuration parameters which allow you to set up their MAC addresses, potentially avoiding this problem.

Host Authentication.   The *host authentication* method allows access to a service based on a source host identifier, which is commonly a network address such as that used by IP, DECnet, X.25 or even the MAC addresses mentioned in the previous section. Figure 4.4 shows a common setup.

Many computer services use host authentication schemes. In a common example, a computer that communicates via X.25 through a serial connection may decide to accept or reject calls based on the source X.121 address. Or, one computer may not allow every computer to access a service, just a subset of all the possible source network addresses.

Because host authentication is based upon network addresses, many network devices also can help accomplish this task. A Token Ring bridge can do so by setting up access restrictions to allow only certain source systems to send data to computers on the other side of the bridge. Packet filters, too, can help accomplish host authentication, although you should not rely on this as the sole method for securing the host.

In another example, a central network management system has a large color display for the network operators to use. Although the many tasks on the network management system may run on multiple computers on the data network, each network management process can display its results on the central system's display. The central system could use host authentication to verify that the computer requesting use of the display is an authorized host. The popular X11 window system uses this strategy. In this case, X servers use host names, which are translated into network addresses, to authorize computers to access the local display.

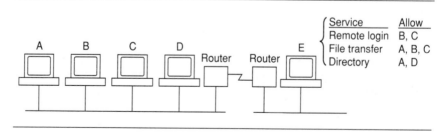

FIGURE 4.4
Computer E uses host authentication to decide the services allowed.

Personal computer file servers often use host authentication to decide which computers will be allowed access to file systems. For example, if a personal computer without a disk is turned on it may request a file system from any file server available. If a particular file server contained sensitive information, you might not want all personal computers using this file system. You could accomplish this by having the file server allow file system access only from authorized personal computers identified by network address.

Host authentication is useful for providing security for some access points, but it is not perfect. If a service on a computer provides access to sensitive information, simply knowing the source host's identity may not be enough qualification for giving out the information. Consider also the following example. Suppose a host named *Trust* offers a service that allows employees to copy programs for company use only. To protect these programs, *Trust* uses host authentication to allow only the host *Innocent* to access the programs. But then suppose a user decides to copy, for personal use, the programs on *Trust*. To do this, the user could turn off *Innocent* and reconfigure the computer *Devious* to have the same network address as *Innocent*. Then, when *Devious* accessed the programs on *Trust,* it would be allowed access because *Trust* thinks *Devious* is *Innocent*.

In another example, suppose a host named *Master* offers a service that allows users to remotely execute software that is under development. As the software on *Master* is not to be shared with every user in the organization, you could use the host authentication method to permit only users on the host *Servant* to execute the program. Let's say that the system administrator of *Servant* assures you that only authorized personnel who can access the new software have accounts on *Servant*. But you are not convinced. You know that relying on the host authentication method means any person who has a valid login on *Servant* can execute the software on *Master*. Thus you decide to boost security for the software on *Master* by going a step further: You employ the user authentication method, which we discuss next.

User Authentication.   *User authentication* offers another method to secure access points by enabling the service to identify each user before allowing that user access. User authentication provides a finer degree of control on a given service than does host authentication because it allows each service to identify the exact user.

A common method used to distinguish users is the password. However, although effective, passwords are not perfect; they are not always as secure as one could hope. One problem with using passwords is that some network services use *cleartext* to transfer the password from the source host to the destination host; using *cleartext* makes it is easy for anyone to discover the passwords by simply capturing packets. A common solution to this problem is to send encrypted passwords, but this method breaks down if the encryption key is broken (although it may take a very long time to break a complicated encryption key).

Another problem associated with employing passwords is that users tend to make them easy to remember, which means they can be easy to discover. Often passwords selected are common words that can be discovered through repeated attempts. The alternative is to provide passwords that are not common words either by randomly generating the passwords or by including in them special characters or digits. Doing this, however, can render them hard to remember, resulting in users writing them down—usually near the host! Despite their drawbacks, passwords still are used frequently to identify users. Engineers simply need to realize their weaknesses and protect against them.

Let's return to our example using *Master* and *Servant* and consider how we could install more effective security management. Instead of allowing every user who has an account on *Servant* to access the software on *Master*, you could use a service that gives access only to those with a valid account on *Master*. Under this arrangement, to run the software from *Master*, a user first would have to start on an authorized host and second, would have to enter a unique password.

In another example, a computer named *Snoopy* provides a service that allows users to access a database consisting of an organization's customer information (see Fig. 4.5). Only employees working in the organization's customer service department are authorized to access this sensitive information.

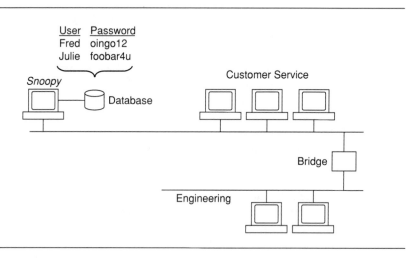

FIGURE 4.5
The service that offers database access on *Snoopy* requires user authentication via a password for each user.

Accordingly, when customer service agents need information about customers, they use a program on their personal computers to connect to *Snoopy*. However, before *Snoopy* gives out information to an agent, the database program asks the agent for a password that identifies that user as authorized to use the database. Thus not every user who walks up to a computer at the desk of a customer service agent can acquire information about customers.

Although user authentication is generally more effective than host authentication used alone, it does have one distinct disadvantage. Nearly all user authentication methods rely on the correct configuration of the computer. Obviously, if the computer provides user authentication for a service, but makes the password the same for every user, the desired security will not be realized.

The combination of host authentication and user authentication provides a more effective means for securing access points than either method used alone. To demonstrate, let's return to our example of *Snoopy*. The method we were going to use was to have each user authorized via a password. But will this provide all the security we need? Any user with a personal computer and a password for an account with database access can access the sensitive information from *Snoopy*. To enhance security we would want to apply both host authentication and user authentication to this service. This two-layered approach will ensure both that users requesting the service come only from authorized hosts and that they are authorized users.

Key Authentication.   A *key authentication* system provides a means to accomplish both host authentication and user authentication with the added advantage of not having to rely solely on the destination host. Key authentication works by assigning a host on the network called a key server.

The *key server* is responsible for issuing keys to authorized users. When a service is requested, the source computer asks the key server for a key. The server then might have the user type in a password for authentication. Now the key server can identify both the source computer and the user requesting the service. Based upon this data, and on the security rules resident within the key server, the server may issue a valid key. This system works because the destination computer will allow the service only if the request for access is accompanied with a valid key. On some key authentication servers, valid keys timeout after a period of time, such as eight hours. This can have the affect of stopping the user's session, but it also ensures that a single valid key does not allow indefinite access. As you can see, because the key server authenticates users and grants access to services, it would need to be under stringent physical security.

A sample request for remote login using key authentication would work as follows (see Fig. 4.6):

1. The source computer (called "source" for short) requests remote login service to the destination computer (called "destination" for short).

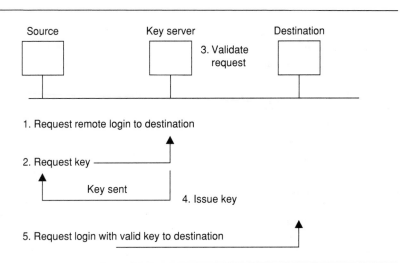

FIGURE 4.6
A sample service request with key authentication.

2. The remote login process requests from the key server a key that allows the user to log in to destination.

3. The key server validates source and ensures the user is authorized to use the remote login service on destination.

4. If all checks out, the key server issues source a valid key for remote login on to destination.

5. Source requests the remote login service from destination with the valid key.

In the key authentication method, the key server is critical for maintaining security on access points to data network services. It is also vitally important that the key server be correctly configured and administered. Note, however, that for key authentication to work, each service on the source computer must request a key from the key server *before* beginning the transaction. Further, the services on the destination computer must accept requests for services only when such requests are accompanied by a valid key. This means that you cannot simply install a key server and start using key authentication. All of your applications and services must also be changed to accommodate using the key server.

Key authentication has become popular in recent years on UNIX computers with the *Kerberos* suite of services from the Massachusetts Institute of Technology. Today, many computer vendors offer some form of key authentication system.

MAINTAINING THE SECURE ACCESS POINTS

The last step in effectively securing network access points is *maintenance*. As we have already seen in some of the examples in this chapter, keeping the security measures on a data network up-to-date and secure is a difficult task requiring an organizational commitment in both time and resources. But just as the engineer must maintain a network no matter how well-planned and well-built it is, inevitably, once the huge task of establishing a security system is complete, maintenance and modification of it will be required.

The key to maintenance is locating potential or actual security breaches. In some cases, this may be done by engineers responsible with auditing network security. They may use as the basis for the audits, for example, the network engineer's documentation of potential network access points and their required security. Unfortunately, keeping such a document current with the wealth of networking software on the market today is another huge task, so in these cases, sometimes the best the auditors can hope for is understanding the issues in security management and the organization's guidelines regarding it.

In other situations, network engineers may deploy programs on hosts to check for commonly known security problems. Simple programs could attempt security breaches by trying passwords and encryption keys at random. More sophisticated programs could launch attacks on the computer network in a variety of ways. In either case, each program would inform the network engineer of its success or failure in breaching security. The logic behind this is that if one program can break a security measure, then another must be able to perform the same feat. The advantage of this approach is that a problem located by a program enables the engineer to close the affected access point, preferably before it is found and exploited by an unauthorized user.

A more unusual approach has been attempted by some more daring organizations: offering on the public networks cash prizes if people can prove they have broken into the organization's network and shown how. While perhaps a bit drastic, this approach does seem to help guarantee security by assisting engineers in locating security breaches.

Unfortunately, no methods suggested here guarantee security will be maintained properly. Audits cannot be performed everyday. Programs that test security cannot check for every possible hole. Network engineers need to understand the security measures in place and make an effort to convey to the organization the necessity of having help in maintaining them.

4.3 Attaching to a Public Network

We described in Section 4.2 the steps involved in accomplishing security management for services on a host. An organization having a data network that does not connect to a public network could find that those steps will provide the necessary security. However, for an organization having a data network that is connected to a public data network, accomplishing security management requires a different approach.

Three types of access are possible from a public data network to an organization's data network:

1. No access
2. Full access
3. Limited access

A private data network that allows no remote login access from a public data network may simply use its connection to a public network as a means of sending and receiving electronic mail. For example, the connection may be established every few hours via a modem for the sole purpose of placing mail onto and receiving mail from the public data network. All transactions with the public data network would be initiated from within the organization's data network. With this method, the organization does not need to find the access points to the public data network, because they do not exist.

In contrast, if an organization places no restrictions on transactions between their computers and a public data network, all security management must reside on each individual computer within the organization. In this setup, the organization may allow any data to enter its network while relying on the computers to provide host authentication and/or user authentication before releasing sensitive information.

However, suppose an organization wants to access some services from a public network or offer some to a public network, but it has no host or user authentication on most of its computers. Obviously, opening itself up to a public network would pose a security risk. The limited access method can help assuage security concerns in this case.

Allowing limited access involves authorizing only a small subset of hosts to provide service between the organization's network and the public network. This popular scenario enables the network engineer to control every computer that offers service to the public data network, thus limiting services available to the public network and better securing access points on the organization's

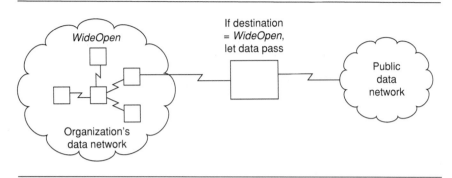

FIGURE 4.7
A setup allowing limited access from the organization's data network to the public data network.

network. For example, let's say the organization has on its data network a machine called *WideOpen,* which is a host on its own physical network segment. Your security setup provides that any data intended for the organization's internal data network must first be sent to *WideOpen* (see Fig. 4.7). You next would want to perform the steps outlined in this chapter to determine the allowable services for *WideOpen.* Often, such services do not include enabling a public network user to use *WideOpen* as a stop-off point before entering the organization's data network. Also, you may want to allow *WideOpen* to act as an electronic mail relay between the public data network and the organization, but not to allow any remote login or file transfer. Using these techniques, you can enable the organization to use the public network without fear of exposing sensitive information to unauthorized users on the public data network. (*NOTE*: The use of host authentication suggested in this example will work unless another computer is mistakenly assigned the same network address as *WideOpen.* However, you can avoid this by assigning to *WideOpen* a network number that is different from that used with the rest of the organization's computers.)

4.4 Security Management on a Network Management System

As we have seen, security management enables network engineers to protect sensitive information by limiting user access to hosts and network resources and by notifying the engineer of attempted or actual breaches of security. This is done by

- identifying the sensitive information to be protected,
- finding the access points,
- securing the access points, and
- maintaining the secure access points.

Security management on a network management system is accomplished through the use of software tools. How well this is done depends on the sophistication of the tool available to the engineer, as we see next when we examine three security management tools.

A SIMPLE TOOL

A simple tool for effecting security management on a network management system would need to show where security measures have been set up. Relying on input from the graphical network map, this tool could produce a screen showing all security measures applicable to any device or host a user selected.

Additionally, to enable you to locate all places in the network that restrict a certain user or network address, the tool should be able to query the configuration database and produce a screen of the necessary information. This security management tool, using the configuration management information already present in the network management system, can be very useful in solving complex connectivity or reachability problems on the network.

A MORE COMPLEX TOOL

The more advanced tool could be designed by including a real-time application that monitors the access points to sensitive information. Upon spotting a potential security problem, this application could change the colors of affected hosts or network devices on the graphical network map. Or, if having too many colors for different events becomes confusing, it could report its findings in some other method designed to catch your attention, such as ringing the system bell and logging its findings in a window that pops up on the network management system automatically (see Fig. 4.8).

For example, such an application could report when a single user has made numerous unsuccessful remote login attempts on a computer. This report could be accomplished in two different ways, depending on the computer's intelligence regarding reporting events. If it can send events to the network management system concerning unsuccessful login attempts, this would be ideal. Otherwise, the security management application would need to have the intelligence to check a computer's log files concerning failed remote login attempts.

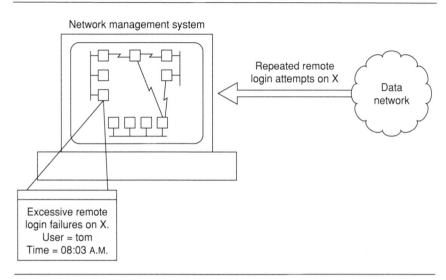

FIGURE 4.8
A real-time security management application reporting many unsuccessful attempts to gain access to the remote login service on computer X.

(Many computers will log failed login attempts in a file for later examination.) Unfortunately, this method requires that the security management application be written to examine specific file formats.

This application could be further developed to produce more useful information, such as reporting repeated denials of user attempts to access a particular service. This reporting would be generated in a manner similar to that described in the previous paragraph.

The tool also could be designed to notify you when an unauthorized user or host attempts to access a service that has an access point to sensitive information. By doing this, the tool could guide you to a needed reconfiguration of a host. For example, suppose a user at a personal computer is requesting file service from an accounting server that holds sensitive information. It is not the intent of the user to gain file service on the accounting server, but on a local server, and perhaps the user doesn't know the necessary configuration to stop the computer from requesting all services available on the network. This tool, monitoring the service access points to the accounting server, could not only advise you of the misguided attempt to gain access, but in the process, alert you to the misconfiguration.

This tool already would bring possible security concerns to the your attention. However, it could also help build security restrictions at points within the network. To do this, you would first select a point on the data network.

Then, you would supply the tool with input about the users or network addresses allowed and denied through the point. Next, the tool would build the correct filters or other measures necessary to produce the desired action. And finally, the tool could confirm the entire process with you.

While the tasks requires of this tool are not complex, a certain amount of sophistication is involved in producing such an application because nearly every different network device or host has a unique method for applying security measures. The tool would first need to query the host or device where security is to be applied and then query the user for the appropriate information. For example, applying security to limit network address traffic is vastly different when performed on either a repeater, bridge, front-end processor, or router. Further, for each device manu- facturer, the application of security can take a completely different form.

AN ADVANCED TOOL

The advanced security management tool would go even further than the com- plex tool and use data gathered concerning traffic patterns to guide you regarding the implications of imposing security. More complete security man- agement requires this functionality as well as the features mentioned for the simple and more complex tools.

The advanced tool would examine the type of security you intend to install on a computer or device and alert you to possible repercussions of such installations. This tool would use input from you in conjunction with historical data to do a full analysis of how a particular security measure would affect the network. For example, let's say you plan to install a host authentication scheme that should stop all traffic between two areas on the data network, *Chaos* and *Ordered* (see Fig. 4.9). This tool would inform you that the planned security would stop 85 percent of the traffic on the data network. Now this percentage effective rate may be the effect you intended; on the other hand, it could be the result of some error in the system or in the design of the scheme. Regardless, the advanced tool would have either reinforced your efforts or warned you about a possible misconfiguration.

4.5 Reporting Security Events

Like real-time applications, audit trails that summarize and report security information are critical to accomplishing security management. With the help of applications that make entries into an audit trail, you can determine patterns of when access points are threatened and hence stop unauthorized access. Also,

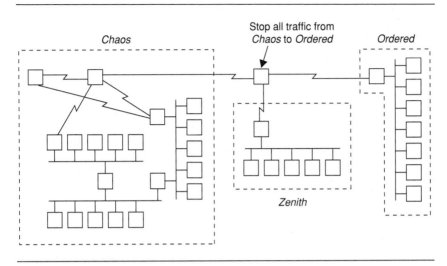

FIGURE 4.9
A security management application could inform the network engineer of the
implication of setting up security to stop all traffic between *Chaos* and *Ordered*.

as with real-time applications, this data can help you find unauthorized requests
that result from misconfiguration.

For example, suppose you are faced with the following situation. Every
day near 2:00 P.M., an unauthorized request for remote login occurs from the
public data network. From this information, you can determine the source
machine, but not a specific user. This source machine belongs to an outside
company. You also can discover that the destination computer within your
network is always the same: *LotsaInfo,* which keeps archives of assorted
information and is part of a service offered to employees to summarize organizational news for each day.

Your first action might be to send an electronic mail message to the
administrators of the source system asking them to watch the system activity
at 2:00 P.M. However, the system has about two hundred users, which could
make watching all outgoing remote login attempts difficult. A few days later,
the source system administrators notify you that they have noticed no unusual
activity around 2:00 P.M. However, your security management application
generating daily summaries continues to show remote login requests to *LotsaInfo* for each day.

Upon further investigation, you discover that the source computer is in the
Eastern time zone of the United States and the destination computer *LotsaInfo,*

resides in the Pacific time zone, a difference of three hours. Two o'clock Pacific time is 5:00 P.M. Eastern time. Now, you ask the source system administrators to check their system near 5:00 P.M. each day for a while, watching for a remote login request to your system. They discern a pattern: Each day near the designated time, a new employee on the computer has been logging in remotely to access a file called 'news-of-the-day' from *LotsaInfo*. Apparently, the new employee transferred to the source system's company recently and had a friend at your company mail him his old configuration files. In the configuration file the user had setup a job that logs into *LotsaInfo* everyday to pick up the 'news-of-the-day' file. After moving to the new company, the user forgot to take out that line and the new system continued to automatically look for that information. This demonstrates that by using the application's summary of unsuccessful login attempts, you would be able to uncover this, while unintentional, potential security breach.

   Producing an application that produces an audit trail is not particularly difficult, provided each security management application that finds potential violations enters its findings in the database on the network management system. For example, an application that discovers numerous unsuccessful remote login attempts also could add an entry into the database when it alerted the network engineer of a problem. The database then could be used to generate the summary reports.

   Although these applications are relatively simple to accomplish with the correct network management system architecture, their usefulness should not be underestimated. Consider the sample daily report shown in Table 4.1.

TABLE 4.1
April 1—Security Summary—Allan's Network

Invalid File Transfer Attempts:

Reported By:	Source:	User:	Time of Day:
Manet	Picasso	Steve	08:03
Manet	Picasso	Steve	08:05
Cezanne	Manet	Julie	08:26
Monet	Rembrandt	James	17:21

Invalid Remote Login Attempts:

Reported By:	Source:	User:	Time of Day:
Renoir	Goya	Carol	08:03
Pissarro	Goya	Jim	12:10
Cezanne	Dali	Alex	12:45
Renoir	Pissarro	Carol	13:26
Pissarro	Monet	????	15:01
Pissarro	Monet	????	15:02
Pissarro	Monet	????	15:03
Cezanne	Manet	guest	15:23
Manet	VanGogh	Steve	18:23

This sample report shows how a security management application can present useful data to network engineers. It identifies two major access points, the invalid attempts found for the day, the source computer, the user name given when the attempt failed (if available), and the time the event occurred. Similar applications that produce relevant data for longer periods, such as a week or month, also are critical to security management on a network management system. Reviewed regularly by the engineer, these reports can help the engineer keep the network secure and be aware of potential or actual security breaches.

Summary

Security management enables the network engineer to control access points to a data network for the purpose of protecting sensitive information from unauthorized access. Protection through security management tools is achieved through specific configuration of network hosts and devices to control access points within the data network but usually does not deal with securing the actual sensitive information. It should not be confused with the different concepts of physical security and operating system security. Its primary benefit is that of securing sensitive information and calming the security concerns of users about attaching hosts to a data network.

Using security management, network engineers can protect sensitive information by limiting the access to hosts and network resources by users and by obtaining reports of attempted or actual breaches of security. It consists of the following four steps:

1. Identifying the sensitive information to be protected,
2. Finding the access points,
3. Securing the access points using such methods as encryption, packet filters, host authentication, user authentication, and key authentication, and
4. Maintaining the secure access points.

Connecting to a public data network provides many opportunities for security breaches against computers attached to a data network. Accordingly, an organization may elect to control public access to its information by allowing either no access, full access, or limited access to the data.

The engineer can use a variety of tools for accomplishing security management. A simple tool can summarize the security barriers set up throughout the data network, while a more complex tool can go further and notify the engineer when a user has attempted access through locked access points. This same tool also could help put the proper mechanisms in place to stop unauthorized access to sensitive information. An advanced tool goes even further and evaluates the implications of putting restrictions on sensitive information based upon historical network traffic information.

For Further Study

Denning, P., *Computers Under Attack: Intruders, Worms and Viruses,* ACM Press, Addison-Wesley Publishing Company, Reading, Mass., 1990.

Hoffman, L. J., *Modern Methods for Computer Security and Privacy,* Prentice-Hall, Englewood Cliffs, New Jersey, 1977.

Shirey, *Security in Local Area Networks,* Proceedings of the Computer Security and Integrity Symposium, December 1982.

Stoll, C., *The Cuckoo's Egg,* Doubleday and Company, Inc., New York, 1989.

5

Performance Management

In this chapter:
- Definition of performance management
- Benefits of the performance management process
- Steps for accomplishing performance management
- Setting of thresholds
- Simulation of the network
- Examples of possible performance management tools
- Flowcharts for performance management tools
- Reporting of performance information

A data network is like a highway on which information travels throughout the organization. And just as a highway you drive on can become chronically congested, so can the capacity of a network highway become overtaxed from the increasing demands of users. Network devices become overloaded, LAN and WAN links become saturated, and consequently, performance suffers.

Performance management involves ensuring this network highway remains accessible and uncrowded so users can utilize it efficiently. It does this by

- monitoring network devices and their associated links to determine utilization and error rates, and
- helping the network provide a consistent level of service to the users by ensuring the capacity of devices and links is not overtaxed to the extent of adversely impacting performance.

It consists of

1. collecting data on current utilization of network devices and links,
2. analyzing relevant data to discern high utilization trends,
3. setting utilization thresholds, and

4. using simulation to determine how the network can be altered to maximize performance.

In this chapter, we present the benefits of performance management and follow with a discussion of the four steps involved in accomplishing it. We then offer you three performance management tools, from simple to advanced, for your consideration. Last, we discuss the methods for reporting performance management information.

5.1 Benefits of the Performance Management Process

The primary benefit of performance management is that it helps the network engineer to reduce network overcrowding and inaccessibility to provide a consistent level of service to users. Using performance management, the engineer can monitor the utilization of network devices and links. The data gathered can help the engineer to determine utilization trends and isolate performance problems, and possibly even solve them before they adversely impact network performance. Performance management also can aid in capacity planning.

Monitoring the current utilization of network devices and links is critical for performance management. The data obtained not only can help you immediately isolate components of the data network that are heavily utilized but also, perhaps more importantly, can help you find answers to other potential problems. For example, users' complaints about slow remote access to a database server could have many probable causes. The problem could lie on any link or device from the source to the destination. Performance management could help you determine quickly that a link between the remote site and the database server is over 80 percent utilized and therefore the likely cause of the slow access (see Fig. 5.1).

Performance management techniques also can assist you in examining network trends. You can use trend data to predict peak network utilization and consequently, to avoid the poor performance that can result from a saturated network.

You also could plot utilization of the network against time to determine times of high usage. Knowing this can help you schedule large data transfers for nonpeak times. For example, on many data networks, users schedule large transfers for after hours when network usage is presumably low. A common time for users to schedule these types of transactions is 12:00 A.M. Although few users may notice a performance problem at that time, network usage can, in fact, reach a fairly high utilization then. Let's say that on such a network, a group plans to transfer each night large graphic images of a circuit board design under development. The people working on this project ask you when the

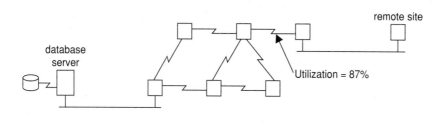

FIGURE 5.1
High utilization of this link causes slow access from the Remote Site to the
Database Server.

optimum time is to deliver these images. Because you have been monitoring
network utilization, you instruct them to transfer at 3:00 A.M. daily, a time that
trend analysis indicated has an average of only five percent utilization.

5.2 Accomplishing Performance Management

Performance management involves the following four steps:

1. Collect data on current utilization of network devices and links.
2. Analyze relevant data.
3. Set utilization thresholds.
4. Simulate the network.

In the next several sections, we examine each of these steps in greater detail.

COLLECTING UTILIZATION DATA

A significant manifestation of over utilization on network devices and links is
a noticeable decrease in the level of service to users. To measure the level of
service, you would want to determine the following:

1. Total response time
2. Rejection rate
3. Availability

Total response time is the amount of time it takes a datum to enter the
network and be processed and then for a response to leave the network. For

example, the total response time for a remote login session can be measured from the time when the user first types a character on the keyboard to the time it takes that information to travel through the network to the destination machine and back again to be displayed back on the local terminal. *Rejection rate* is the percentage of time the network cannot transfer information because of a lack of resources and performance. *Availability* is the percentage of time the network is accessible for use and operational and is often measured as *mean time between failure*, or *MTBF*.

You could use a network management protocol to collect this data from the network. You will find that this information can be important both for real-time troubleshooting of the network and for trend analysis.

ANALYZING THE DATA

Your analysis could result in a graphical representation of the utilization of a network device or link either in real-time or from a historical perspective. For example, you could use line or bar graphs, which are most useful for performance analysis.

Real-time graphical analysis is instrumental in troubleshooting network performance problems because it can show current network usage or errors, as seen in Fig. 5.2.

Graphs that plot historical data for the network won't show you the current status of the network but are useful for illustrating trends. Trend data can help you evaluate when the user demand for the network will exceed a device's or link's capacity. A graph can show not only the increase or decrease of utilization

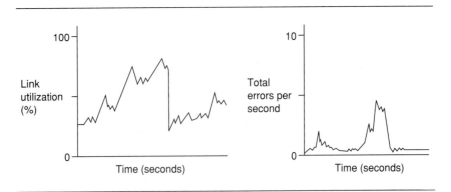

FIGURE 5.2
Real-time graphs of network link utilization and total errors are useful for troubleshooting performance problems

on a network link but also other useful statistics such as error rates on a link and processor usage for a device for a given time period. Further, using monthly, quarterly, and yearly trends, you can plan more easily for future network capacity.

SETTING THRESHOLDS

Another step in the performance management process is the setting of utilization thresholds. You can set threshold on a variety of items that can affect network performance. For a network device or host these may include processor utilization, alarm durations, and so forth. On a link you may choose to set thresholds on items such as error rate, average utilization, and overall throughput.

Once thresholds are set, performance management tools can report to the engineer when the performance of the network reaches a certain error rate or utilization. Determining the value to set as a threshold may be difficult; however, most often, you will find that trial and error will produce a reasonable value. Thresholds can enable you to locate and fix a problem before it affects network performance. Combining the graphical presentation of the utilization data with utilization thresholds is a powerful tool for accomplishing performance management.

USING NETWORK SIMULATION

Network simulation is yet another performance management tool you can use. With this tool, you can be better assured that the network you build will perform to the expectations of users.

Note, building the model for network simulation is a difficult task (few software companies today can simulate complex network configurations). For this reason, this text does not cover how to build a network simulation system. Instead, we address how to use network simulation to accomplish performance management.

You can employ simulation to determine how to alter a network for more efficient use and higher performance. For example, consider an example of a network's remote site where users are experiencing poor response time. Often, this poor response time results from a heavily congested link. Let's say that upon investigating the usage of the link to the remote site, you find it averages over 80 percent utilization. Consequently, you decide to upgrade the bandwidth of the link. Yet, after the upgrade, users at the remote site are still experiencing poor response time. Searching further, you find that the network device connecting the site cannot handle traffic at a rate faster than the rate the older link produced. Thus upgrading the link did not solve the poor response problem. Running a simulation of the network before upgrading the link probably could have helped you detect this deficiency with the network device.

5.3 Performance Management on a Network Management System

Performance management on a network management system involves using intelligent tools that can examine the state of the network in both a real-time and a historical perspective. As with the other types of network management we have discussed, the effectiveness of performance management depends on the level of tool available to the engineer, as we see next when we examine three levels of performance management tools.

A SIMPLE TOOL

A simple tool for performance management should provide real-time information about network devices and links, preferably in graphical form such as a line or bar graph. This level tool can help you find network bottlenecks and isolate performance problems.

For network devices, the simple tool also should provide data about processor and memory utilization. High processor utilization may mean a device cannot handle the network traffic, while excessive memory utilization may mean a device is buffering vast amounts of data. A real-time graph of these values can alert you to a potential performance problem with the device, as seen in Fig. 5.3.

On network links, the simple tool also should be able to show you current utilization and error rates. For example, a graph of packets per second and bits per second for the link is useful for showing overall link performance. Another useful value to graph is the current utilization of the network link, found by dividing the rate of bits per second on the link by the maximum bits per second. In a troubleshooting situation, you may want to examine the number of errors on a link versus the amount of good data sent. The simple tool could overlay these two graphs and produce the necessary result for you.

A MORE COMPLEX TOOL

A complex tool would go a step further than the simple version by allowing you to set thresholds for utilization and error rates. Then if the network exceeded those thresholds, the tool could perform a prescribed action, which we discuss further in the next paragraph. This level of tool also could gather real-time information and store it in a database management system, which can be used to do historical studies and produce graphs, like those seen in the simple tool, to view the past performance of the network.

Setting thresholds that can trigger a subsequent action provides considerable functionality to the engineer. The tool should enable you to specify the action. This action you select could be simple, such as ringing a bell or flashing

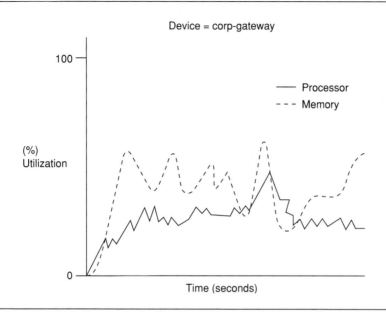

FIGURE 5.3
Functionality of the simple tool.

a light, or more advanced, such enabling a backup circuit, calling a pocket paging system, or sending electronic mail. For example, in many parts of the world Switched 56 or ISDN services offer high bandwidth circuits on demand using a special modem or adapter. The billing of these dialed circuits is based on time, thus making the circuits cost-effective for periods of high use on network resources. The tool could use this technology to dial a new circuit based on utilization, error rates, or any threshold set by the network engineer.

A threshold is vital to the functionality of the complex tool; however, you can go further to optimize this facility. The complex tool could warn you not only about an incident that crosses a threshold but also about a situation where the threshold is neared. For example, the tool may be set up to monitor the utilization of a processor on a network device. Suppose that on a certain device, the point where the processor utilization affects network performance is 90 percent of total capacity. The tool could be set up to notify you when the processor utilization reached 80 percent of this threshold, thus allowing you to examine the network as a performance problem is occurring.

Further, the tool should be able to re-arm the threshold in a reasonable manner. Suppose a threshold is set to ring an alarm when utilization reaches 60 percent, which if exceeded, prompts the alarm to sound. Then, an instant later the utilization drops to 58 percent. The alarm stops. A few seconds later, the utilization reaches 61 percent, causing another alarm to sound. You easily can see how this progression of multiple alarms can become redundant and annoying. The tool should be set up so that when the threshold is reached the first time, the tool sets off an alarm. Subsequently, the tool would re-arm the threshold only if the utilization dropped below another defined value, such as 40 percent (see Fig. 5.4). With this arrangement, the tool would sound an alarm when the threshold is exceeded; another alarm would sound only if the utilization dropped below 40 percent and then proceeded to again exceed 60 percent.

Flowchart 5.1 demonstrates this example. The tool could be set up to use this same concept for checking error rates on network links as well.

The more complex tool also should be able to graph the historical performance management data placed into the database management system. When a

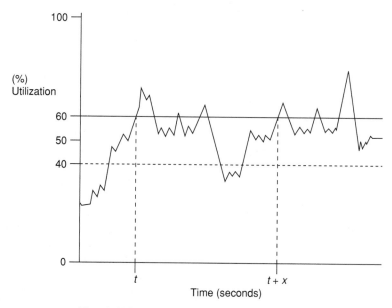

Threshold for alarm: 60%
Re-arm alarm at: 40%

FIGURE 5.4
An example of the complex tool. For the utilization graphed, an alarm rings twice, at time t and time $t + x$.

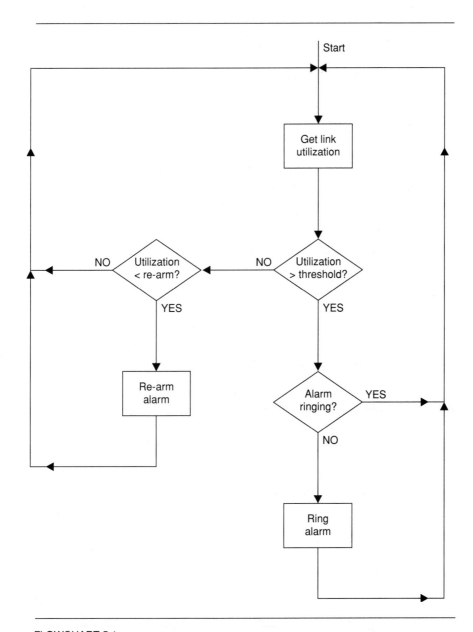

FLOWCHART 5.1
This flowchart is for a tool that checks link utilization and rings an alarm based upon threshold and re-arm values.

data network experiences a performance problem, often the engineer can't simultaneously examine all relevant aspects. Further, in many cases the user may complain about the problem at some time subsequent to its occurrence. In these situations, the real-time graphing ability of the simple tool can't help you. However, being able to retrieve the necessary information and then examine it in graphical format can significantly help in resolving this type of problem.

The tool should produce various graphs including line, bar, and pie. Line graphs are useful for examining trends in data, such as utilization. Bar graphs are effective for showing one value in comparison to another, such as memory consumed on a network device versus the number of packets handled. Pie graphs are valuable for demonstrating the percentage of values; for example, you may find helpful a pie graph of the types of traffic passing through a network device during periods of slow performance. Examples of each graph format are shown in Fig. 5.5.

Let's examine further how graphs can help you in performance management. Suppose two users are logged into two personal computers on a token ring network, *Gatsby* and *Daisy*. *Gatsby* and *Daisy* use the token ring to share an application that clerks need in order to enter sales and order processing information prior to a nightly download to the company's mainframe. At seemingly random times, the users experience a brief period of interrupted service where no data seems to pass on the token ring network.

This is a common scenario. To help isolate the problem, you first could have the performance management tool graph the error rate on the token ring network segment for the last two days. Let's say a line graph shows a very small number of errors occurring within normal operating specifications. Because the error rate on the ring is apparently not the problem, you then could have the tool produce a line graph of the utilization of the ring for the same period. This graph shows peak utilization just before 12:00 P.M., at 3:00 P.M., and at 12:00 A.M., all of which correspond to times when the network is busiest and system backups are most likely to occur. However, the users report they are experiencing performance problems at times other than these peak times.

Accordingly, you could rightly conclude that this problem doesn't lie within the token ring network itself. Next, you could graph the processor utilization of both *Gatsby* and *Daisy*. Suppose that the graph shows many times during the past two days when the utilization peaked at 100 percent. You then could ask the users on the hosts if they were doing any processor-intensive operations during these periods of inadequate performance. Both state that at those times, they were simply typing in information that feeds the order processing application.

Because the application running on the personal computers most likely is not causing the processor load to skyrocket, you realize that some other outside influence must be the cause of the problem. Now, you know that most manufacturers can potentially speak a different network protocol, so examining the

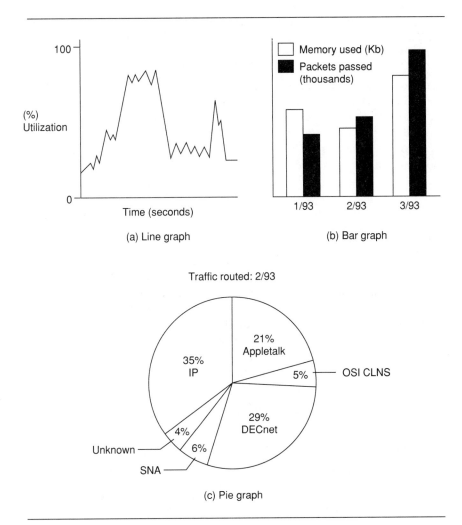

(a) Line graph

(b) Bar graph

Traffic routed: 2/93

(c) Pie graph

FIGURE 5.5
Types of graphs produced by the complex tool.

types of traffic on the token ring that the personal computers see may shed some light on the problem. Therefore you next could have the tool make pie charts showing the percentage of different types of traffic on the token ring. To accomplish this, you have the tool query *Daisy* and *Gátsby* at five-minute intervals and make a chart for the types of traffic they observe.

After a few hours, you examine the charts. Some show a wide distribution of different network protocols on the token ring; however, others show that a protocol not understood by either *Gatsby* or *Daisy* dominates the token ring. Further analysis reveals that the times when the processor load hit 100 percent on *Gatsby* and *Daisy* correlate exactly to when the network protocol they don't understand contributed a major portion of traffic to the token ring. Your final step, then, would be to determine why the two personal computers react poorly to the foreign network protocol. You find that the protocol uses specific token ring packets to locate network services (printers, file servers, routers, etc.) and so conclude that for some reason, *Gatsby* and *Daisy* react poorly to these packets. As a possible temporary solution, you finally could move these computers to another token ring segment until the true cause of the problem can be uncovered.

AN ADVANCED TOOL

The advanced tool would offer functionality beyond that of the complex tool, specifically regarding the exploration of the past state of the network; the prediction of response time, rejection rate, and availability; and network simulation.

Examining the Network's Historical Data.   The advanced tool should be able to use information found in the relational database to examine the state of the network at any point in the past to look for probable performance problems and aid in capacity planning. To accomplish this task, the tool would need to be able to

- receive user input about the state of the network and performance problems,
- retrieve information from the database, and
- analyze the state of the network.

The first step of this process requires that you tell the tool at what time in the past it should examine the data on the network. You also would need to tell the tool which hosts, devices, or links it should look at. For example, you could instruct the tool to review the performance between two hosts on the network for the previous month.

Next, the tool would need to retrieve information on the network management system from the relational database. For each element it is to examine, the tool would need to know what information to extract. For example, on a network device the tool could gather processor, buffer, and memory utilization; for a network link, the tool could fetch data about error rates and bandwidth utilization. Note, you should be able to specify any additional information the tool is to obtain from the database.

The tool then would analyze this data to determine the source of a particular performance problem. It would examine predefined events such as high error rates, an incident of a threshold being exceeded, or an overall increase in traffic. Using the Structured Query Language (SQL), you could add rules to the analysis; for example, the following statement adds the rule to look for a host with more than 10 users:

```
SELECT * FROM hosts WHERE users > 10
```

In another example, the advanced tool could help you to perform capacity planning for network links with information from the relational database. When network links become utilized above a certain percentage they can affect network performance. This percentage can differ dramatically depending on the intended use of the link and the response time the users require. A common problem is that once you discover that a link has reached its critical utilization percentage, it often takes a long time to upgrade the link to one with more bandwidth. At the time of this writing, if you have to order a new link from a circuit vendor this period could be around 45 days.

The advanced tool can use information from the relational database to help you predict when a link will surpass the critical utilization threshold in advance. Thus, you can start to upgrade the link and have it installed before the users see a performance problem.

To begin, the tool must have input from you concerning how long it typically takes to upgrade a link and at what percentage utilization the users begin to see a performance problem. For example, you may tell the tool it takes you 45 days to install a new link and at 60 percent utilization users begin to see a performance problem when transmitting information across the link.

The relational database should have information that allows the tool to compute the average utilization of a link for each hour since it became operational. To gather this information the tool would have to poll the interface on a network device that connects to the link at least once an hour and note the link's current utilization.

Once this information was in the relational database, the advanced tool could internally compute the trend of the actual utilization and project when the utilization will surpass your set threshold, as seen in Figure 5.6. If this projected time is less than or equal to the time it takes to upgrade a link, the tool should warn you that it is time to start the upgrade. For instance, if the tool measures the utilization of a link at 23 percent and notices that if the utilization continues to increase at its current rate it will surpass the 60 percent threshold in 45 days, it should warn you. It may do this by sending an electronic mail message or bringing up a message on the network management system.

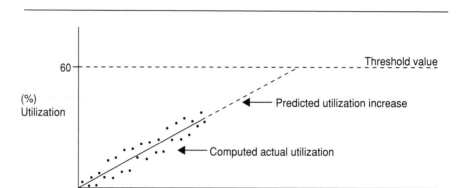

FIGURE 5.6
The current actual utilization trend shows that the link utilization will surpass
the 60 percent threshold. The tool should warn the network engineer in
enough time to allow the upgrade of the link to be performed before users see
a performance problem.

The advanced tool could save you significant amounts of time while
assisting you in drawing conclusions about areas on the network that could
experience unacceptable performance. (Note that this tool potentially can
consume large quantities of storage. You would want to decide the extent of
historical information to save and provide the necessary storage for it.)

In another example, suppose you receive input that users transferring data
from the computer *Mars* to the computer *Venus* have been encountering slow
performance over the past week. Figure 5.7 shows the applicable network configuration. You could have the tool analyze the portion of the network that intercon-
nects *Mars* and *Venus*. Let's say the analysis reveals that the error rate on a link
connecting two remote bridges on the path between the two computers has been
steadily increasing. This rate has increased enough to warrant examination, but
not enough to trigger a threshold alarm. Using the features described earlier
this section, the advanced tool could produce a line graph to show this error
rate progression, thus enabling you to call the circuit vendor and report the
problem with less time wasted than if you had not had the tool.

Simulating the Network.   In addition to examining the past state of the
network, the advanced tool should help you analyze future performance and

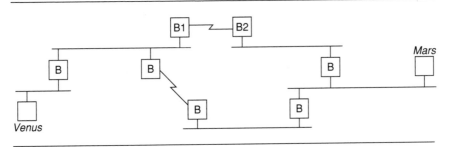

FIGURE 5.7
The advanced tool quickly analyzes the problem: an increasing error rate on
the link between B1 and B2.

determine what configuration can produce the greatest performance. This could
be done using network simulation, where the tool would take input data from
the running network or simulation and make predictions concerning users'
perceptions of the network's performance.

Predicting Response Time, Rejection Rates, and Availability. Given sufficient input, the tool also should be able to simulate traffic and show probable
response times, rejection rates, and availability, thus helping you to purchase the
proper network devices and allocate the correct bandwidth.

This feature can be particularly useful when you are building a data
network because it can help you ensure that the network performs optimally
and helps you possibly avoid future problems. For example, suppose a new site
wishes to connect to a network. The users expect a response time of less than
half of a second, nearly zero rejection rate, and 100 percent availability for the
connection between their site and a remote sales office. Using the advanced
tool, you could model various links from the new site using different speed
links and then prepare the model with the appropriate number of network
devices and hosts.

5.4 Reporting Performance Information

Many methods are available for reporting performance data. The most common
format is a text report. This type of report, which can be displayed on nearly
any computer and can be easily printed, typically shows the utilization and error
rates for network devices, as shown in Table 5.1.

TABLE 5.1
REPORT FOR MAY, 1992

Network device:	% Utilization		% Errors	
	Average:	Peak:	Average:	Peak:
Dallas-GW	6	23	1	1
Phoenix-Bridge	12	13	4	5
New York-GW	23	56	8	12
Houston-GW	42	78	12	22
New Jersey-Bridge	3	10	0	0
Corp-HUB	12	54	1	3

While the above report is useful for obtaining performance management information for network devices, generating a similar report for network links is also worthwhile, as shown in Table 5.2.

A text report can contain valuable information. However, as we have discussed in this chapter, it can be beneficial to represent performance management information in a graph; therefore, ideally, the software would be able to turn such reports into graphs.

The bitmapped display found on network management systems provides another method for graphical representation of the data. Many imaginative methods exist for reporting performance management information via such a display. For example, you could set up the display so that as the utilization of a link increases, its picture appears thicker or changes color on the network map. The picture for a network link experiencing errors could flash; that for a network link experiencing a large error rate could be represented by a broken line.

The bitmapped display offers the same advantages for network devices. For example, as devices increase in utilization, their picture on the network map could grow larger; that for a device with excessive utilization could appear to perspire; and that representing a network device that has seen an increase in error rate could develop a crack. By taking advantage of the bitmapped display, you could tell at a glance the general performance of the network links and devices.

Summary

Performance management involves ensuring the data network remains accessible so users can utilize it efficiently. It accomplishes this by monitoring the utilization of network devices and their associated links and ensuring the

TABLE 5.2
REPORT FOR MAY, 1992

Network link:	% Utilization		% Errors	
	Average:	Peak:	Average:	Peak:
Dallas-Houston	4	8	0	1
New York-New Jersey	22	64	3	14
Corp-Seattle	56	69	12	62
Corp-Houston	56	83	2	5
Phoenix-Houston	12	21	0	0

capacity of devices and links is not overtaxed to the extent of adversely impacting performance.

This form of network management consists of the following four steps: (1) collecting data on current utilization of network devices and links, (2) analyzing relevant data to discern high utilization trends, (3) setting utilization thresholds, and (4) using network simulation to determine how the network can be altered to maximize performance. Performance management is beneficial in that it helps prevent network overcrowding and inaccessibility and thus aids in providing a consistent level of service to users. For the engineer, it provides the means to collect and analyze data on performance, to set utilization thresholds, and to arrange for warning messages when thresholds are near or at capacity. It also assists the engineer in planning for future capacity.

The engineer can use a number of tools for accomplishing performance management on a network management system. A simple tool can monitor the real-time performance of network devices and produce graphs for engineer review. A more complex tool further can capture performance management data in a database and present it in the form of graphs for later review. It also provides the means of setting thresholds to help monitor the network and allows the setting of alarms based upon those thresholds. An advanced tool for performance management would offer, in addition to the functionality of the complex tool, the advantage of allowing historical analysis and the means to perform network simulation.

Various methods for reporting performance information are available. While text reports are the most common way to format these reports, representing the data in either a graphical format or on a bitmapped display also can be of great help to the network engineer.

For Further Study

Daigle, A., *Queuing Theory for Telecommunications,* Addison-Wesley Publishing Company, Reading, Mass., 1990.

Fortier, P., and G. Desrochers, *Modeling and Analysis of Local Area Networks,* CRC Press, Boca Raton, Fl., 1990.

Greiner, R., and G. Metes, *Enterprise Networking,* Digital Press, Digital Equipment Corporation, 1992.

Schwartz, M., *Telecommunication Networks: Protocols, Modeling and Analysis,* Addison-Wesley Publishing Company, Reading, Mass., 1987.

6

Accounting Management

In this chapter:
- Definition of accounting management
- Benefits of the accounting management process
- Steps for accomplishing accounting management
- Billing of network users
- Examples of possible accounting management tools
- Flowcharts for accounting management tools
- Reporting of accounting information

Accounting management involves measuring the usage of network resources by users in order to establish metrics, check quotas, determine costs, and bill users.

It includes

- gathering data about the utilization of network resources,
- setting usage quotas using metrics, and
- billing users for their use of the network.

Accounting management is the process of gathering network statistics. The gathering of these statistics can help the network engineer make decisions regarding the allocation of network resources. Likewise, these numbers are useful in managing system resources such as disk space, processing power, and backup storage even though these are not necessarily a part of network management.

In this chapter, we examine first the benefits of accounting management and next the steps involved in achieving it. We include a detailed discussion of network billing and then offer three accounting management tools for you to consider. Last, we examine methods for reporting accounting information.

6.1 Benefits of the Accounting Management Process

The primary benefit of accounting management is that it enables the engineer to measure and report accounting information based on individual and group users and then use this data to bill those users, allocate resources, and compute the cost, by user, of transmitting data across the network. It has the added benefit of adding to the engineer's understanding of user utilization of network resources, which can help in the creation of a more productive network.

Billing users obviously is essential for recovering expenses involved in building and maintaining the data network. Accounting management not only can provide for this but, coupled with billing policy, can help provide for fair distribution of these costs. It further can assist in budget and personnel planning. Often, an organization views these vital aspects of accounting management as the most important.

By examining metrics and quotas, you can ensure that each user has sufficient resources to accomplish required tasks. You also could use these statistics to track the usage of various networked resources such as application servers, compute servers, file servers, and print servers. For example, a documentation group may use the network to access a desktop publishing system on an application server at a remote site. Using accounting management information, you find that majority of the traffic across the network to the remote site is the documentation group accessing this application server. This may or may not be a resource issue for the network, but accounting management provides the information that allows you to make a decision as to whether or not the documentation group warrants their own application server.

In a traditional network environment that relies on modem connections to a central host, accounting management can help you allocate time in a time-share situation for a group of terminals, as illustrated in Fig. 6.1. Certain users might have priority use on the terminals. Accounting management can assist in your determination whether these users actually use the terminals a large percentage of the time or if the priority scheme needs modification.

This data further can influence the distribution of valuable resources. For example, consider a situation in which a network site consists of many distributed personal computer file servers. These servers contribute multiple functions on the network, ranging from print spoolers to database servers. One file server, *Hercules,* contains important stock market information in a database. Suppose then that a user of this file server decides to back up his or her entire personal computer 40-megabyte disk onto *Hercules.* The user starts the backup and then leaves the office for the night. After the backup procedure finishes, only one megabyte of storage remains on *Hercules.* Early the next morning, *Hercules* executes a program that gathers important stock information from another server; however, while downloading this data, *Hercules's* disk becomes full and the transfer halts.

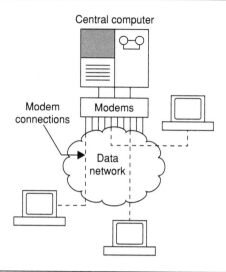

FIGURE 6.1
Accounting management helps keep track of which users and groups access the terminals that connect via modem to the central computer. This information can help the network engineer make decisions about the allocation of network resources.

A few hours later when people attempt to retrieve the important stock information, they receive an error message. In investigating the problem, you examine the accounting management statistics for *Hercules* and notice that a user downloaded a number of files that took a long period during the night. You now have some options depending on your own network operational procedures. You may elect to contact the user or forward the information you learned via accounting management to the system administrator of *Hercules* for appropriate action.

Accounting management techniques also can help organizations compute the cost for sending data across the data network for a given user, which enables the user to see how much money they are spending to get the network services. This provides fair distribution of the costs associated with running and maintaining the network.

6.2 Accomplishing Accounting Management

Accounting management consists of the following steps:

1. Gather data about the utilization of network resources.
2. Use metrics to help set usage quotas.

3. Bill users for their use of the network.

We examine each of these in the next several sections.

GATHERING DATA ABOUT NETWORK UTILIZATION

To obtain information about metrics and quotas, you might find that you need to gather accounting management data only infrequently. You might determine that you need to retrieve billing data more often, but if network devices can store a sufficient amount of activity data, periodic retrieval of data might suffice.

SETTING QUOTAS

Metrics can assist you in learning to what extent users employ network resources. For example, a metric can reveal the number of connections made to a terminal server, the number of transactions made with a particular database, or the total login time by a user to a supercomputer. As part of utilizing accounting management, you would want to decide which network resources to measure and then begin collecting metrics concerning their use.

Metrics work with quotas to help ensure each user gets a "fair share" of network resources. You might elect to set up quotas and then penalize users for exceeding those quotas, for instance, by denying them use of the network resource in question.

Commonly, a data network is employed by users to access a large computer with a database of information. The company that has the data base might then charge the user for this access. Consider for example a company that maintains a large law library online; the network setup for this example is shown in Fig. 6.2. Users pay an access fee and for dial-up connections to the library. Each participant on the network is allowed to use the library for 10 hours each week. This might seem like a short amount of time. However, this is not necessarily the case because the service allows users to login, search the library for data, and then download pages of information; the connection time is used searching for data and transferring information and not for casual perusal of the library contents.

The organization offering the service has determined that the metric of 10 hours is reasonable for most users. A user exceeding this quota will pay a larger monthly fee based on how much time over 10 hours they use.

Let's say you are the network engineer who runs this service. You would want to monitor the users who connect to their modems. Terminal servers would then connect the modems to the main network where the database machines reside. You could query the terminal servers on an hourly basis to learn who

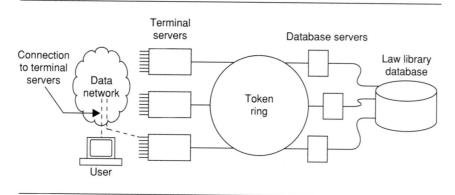

FIGURE 6.2
Users access the law library database through modem connections to
terminal servers.

has connected and for what duration. Based upon this information, you could
then determine the large users of the database and compute the average connection time per user and the time period during which the highest volume of
calls are received.

BILLING USERS

Usually, you will want to collect billing data regularly. Most network devices
have statistical counters that enable you to poll the device for information
relatively infrequently and then note the changes since the last poll. To help
you accomplish this, the network device could keep an accounting table that
records source/destination address pairs in conjunction with the number of
transactions, packets, or bytes sent between them.

Users often are billed based on one of the following scenarios:

1. One-time installation fee and monthly fees
2. Fee based on amount of network resources consumed

One-time Installation Fee and Monthly Fees.   Under this scenario, the
user is billed for the installation of the network connection and then a standard
fee for each month of use. Using this method, accounting management is not
necessary for billing. Although this is the easiest system to implement, it can
become hard to justify why one user who continually utilizes the network is
billed the same amount as is the casual user.

Fee Based on Amount of Network Resources Consumed. The second plan calls for billing each user based on their consumption of network resources. Some organizations use this technique in conjunction with charging small installation and monthly fees. Implementing this technique requires statistics on per user network utilization. The following criteria, used individually or in combination, could be measured to determine network resource usage:

a) Total number of transactions

b) Total packets

c) Total bytes

In the case of measuring total bytes or packets, measurement could be based either on user input to the network or user output from the network.

a) By counting the total number of transactions per user, an organization can measure a several different criteria, including the number of logins to a compute server, of connections made to a terminal cluster controller, of electronic mail messages sent, remote login sessions established, and so forth. An example of this billing design is shown in Fig. 6.3.

Although this design has the advantage of being relatively easy to implement, it carries the following disadvantage: Each transaction results in the same amount charged regardless of the time or resources used. Thus if one user makes a single transaction that sends five hundred megabytes of information, that user is billed the same as the user that sends a one-hundred-byte mail message. Many users probably would object to such a billing strategy.

b) Counting the total number of packets produces bills that reflect actual network usage. Every time a user sends or receives a packet, the bill increases. This method has one drawback: The bill for a given number of packets is the same regardless of the amount of information sent or received.

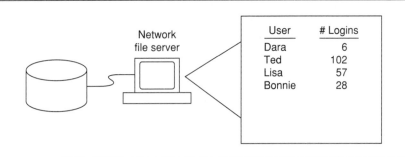

FIGURE 6.3
One billing model calls for charging users based on the number of logins to a compute server. Each login denotes a use of network resources.

For example, one user might send small packets for interactive traffic that do not burden the network devices or links. At the same time, another user initiates a file transfer that relies on large packets. If both the interactive traffic and the file transfer need one thousand packets to complete, their bills would match. However, that's not the way it works: The file transfer with its larger packets will utilize more network resources and yet be billed the same as the interactive traffic, which uses fewer resources.

c) The disadvantages of the first two methods can be avoided by instead billing total bytes used. With this method, the consumer is billed based on the amount of network resources used. The next decision to make is whether to bill total bytes sent or received. (Billing on total traffic in both directions is redundant in nearly all network configurations.) There are clear advantages to both policies.

Billing on bytes sent to the data network intuitively makes sense—when a user sends something across the network, their bill should increase. Unfortunately, in the client/server model of networking prevalent today, this billing structure has some serious flaws. Billing on output tends to discourage users from offering services from their own servers. To illustrate, suppose one user on the network has a file server that contains important data for a research project. Many users connect to the file server and download vast amounts of information daily. Those who gather information send small packets to the servers requesting information. The file server then transfers large amounts of data back to the user, as illustrated in Fig. 6.4. If billing is based on output

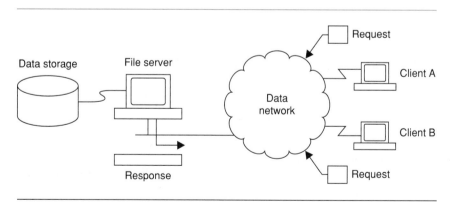

FIGURE 6.4
The file server receives small requests from the clients and returns large responses. Billing the bytes sent to the network results in the group that runs the file service getting a large bill.

bytes, the user offering the information will receive a large bill which, in turn, causes the user who runs the file server to bill its users in an effort to recover their expenses.

Alternatively, users could be billed based on bytes received from the data network. This method eliminates the problem of users who have servers paying for their clients' receipt of information. There is no bill for sending large amounts of data to the network, only for receiving it.

In a classic network setup in which billing on bytes received is appropriate, consider a central site that has a large mainframe computer, *Hulk*. Users connect to *Hulk* through a front-end processor, which connects to a series of cluster controllers with terminals scattered throughout the world via low bandwidth dedicated data links. Smaller packets are sent from the terminals to *Hulk;* larger dumps of information are received back from *Hulk* to the terminal.

Users in many network environments can configure a host to allow access to certain files without explicit permission being required. On IP (Internet Protocol) networks, one method to accomplish this is through anonymous FTP (file transfer protocol). For Appletalk networks, the same effect is achieved through sharing of folders. On a Novell file server, a directory can be left unsecured for clients to deposit or retrieve data. Most of these services are designed to establish a central location for users to pick up documents and applications. By billing bytes received from the network, a company can help ensure a user offering a service does not automatically receive a large bill.

Billing bytes received does have some flaws. First, many network protocols send acknowledgements from the destination to the source, resulting in users who offer services to the network receiving bytes of data from the network that they did not request. Fortunately, acknowledgement packets are usually quite small. These bytes could be ignored, however, by network devices that can compute the total number of acknowledgements seen. Also, the organization that computes the bills can recognize the users who offer services to the network and possibly offer them a discount on their bills.

Another problem with billing based on bytes received is that unsolicited network data, such as electronic mail, adds to the user's bill. This flaw can perhaps be overlooked because many users send and receive mail on the same order of magnitude. This might not be the case, however, when a user is on a mailing list and receives many mail messages. In this situation, the user is on the mailing list for a reason and their bill should reflect the receipt of this data as a result of this network service.

Still another possible imperfection in this billing method arises from each user receiving data from the network as the organization monitors it for management reasons, as illustrated in Fig. 6.5. However, much of this data will be sent to the user regularly, in a pattern, and for a given time period—queries might come once a day or an hour or every few minutes. It's possible to compute

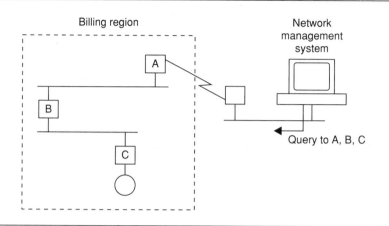

FIGURE 6.5
The queries from the network management system can add to the number of bytes a billing region receives. This, in turn, adds to the total bill.

how many queries are sent typically in the billing period and how many bytes they comprise; for example, if the organization bills monthly, you easily could compute the number of queries on average sent in a given month and subtract these bytes from each bill. In theory all other bytes sent for management reasons should occur while an engineer is troubleshooting network problems, which is a service to the user.

When implementing a resource-based billing scheme, accounting management is necessary to gather the needed statistics. This then requires the organization to get the resource information, process it, and produce the bills based upon the resources consumed.

6.3 Accounting Management on a Network Management System

As we have seen, accounting management enables network engineers to measure the usage of network resources to establish metrics, check quotas, determine costs, and bill users. This is done by

1. gathering data about the utilization of network resources,
2. setting usage quotas with the aid of metrics, and
3. billing users for their use of the network.

How well accounting management accomplishes these functions depends on the level of tool available to the engineer. We next examine three tools that can be used to achieve this facet of network management.

A SIMPLE TOOL

The simple tool should enable you to monitor for any metric that exceeds a quota. The metric data would be stored in the relational database that is part of the network management system architecture and the metric itself would be configurable by the engineer. To determine if quotas have been passed, you would use an SQL query and the tool would show the results of the query.

For example, let's say you need to monitor the number of users on an application server. You could instruct the simple tool to query the application server once every hour, determine the number of users, and then place that data into the relational database. Next, you could instruct the simple tool to look in the relational database by using the following SQL statement:

```
SELECT time, number-users FROM system-statistics
```

The simple tool then would show the number of users each hour using the application server. The results of this SQL query are shown in Table 6.1. Because the metric data would be stored in the relational database, these statistics could be displayed and used in a number of ways, including establishing metrics and quotas for the maximum number of users logged onto this application server.

Similarly, you might want to know when a user has had more than three unsuccessful login attempts via the network to a financial database. You could have the tool monitor this statistic by instructing it to query the financial database server hourly for all unsuccessful remote login attempts. The simple tool would then store this information in the relational database. The following

TABLE 6.1

Time	Number of Users
8:00 A.M.	6
9:00 A.M.	21
10:00 A.M.	22
11:00 A.M.	20
12:00 P.M.	8

SQL query would produce the necessary accounting information from the database bad-logins table:

```
SELECT user, number-attempts FROM bad-logins WHERE
number-attempts > 3
```

Accordingly, the tool would give you the user's name and the number of that users invalid login attempts, if more than three, as illustrated in Table 6.2.

A MORE COMPLEX TOOL

A more complex tool should enable you to perform network billing. Implementing a billing process on a data network can be extremely difficult and time consuming. The complex tool should alleviate this burden by taking as input the topology of the data network and the billing domains and then computing the necessary bills for users.

The complex tool would need data from both the network management system and the engineer to perform its functions. It should be able to obtain the network topology from the network management system relational database. Further, because the hierarchial map of the network management system is in the database, this information also would be available to the tool. Next, the tool must be able to understand how the logical topology of the network is broken up into billing domains, a step that would also require engineer input.

One way to accomplish this task is for you to use the mouse on the network management system to denote a billing region on the network map. You would place the mouse on the map and size a rectangle to surround a group of network devices, hosts, and links. This would be where the tool should poll. For example, a group to be billed has hosts that reside behind a single network device. The tool would compute this fact and poll the single network device for the necessary statistics.

TABLE 6.2

Remote User	Number of Unsuccessful Logins
Norm	4
Cliff	5
Frazier	12
Woody	5
Paul	4

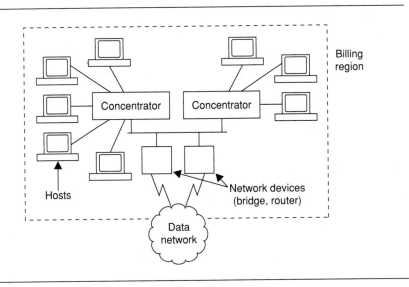

FIGURE 6.6
All the hosts in this billing region connect to one of two 10 BaseT concentrators.
The more complex tool discovers this and polls the concentrators for
billing information.

Going a step further, the tool itself would be able to determine where to
poll for billing information. Consider a network that consists of many hosts on
a LAN, as seen in Fig. 6.6. Each of these hosts is connected to the LAN via a
twisted pair (10baseT) concentrator. Using the network map, you would select
a region that denotes a single floor of an office building, where all the hosts
happen to connect to one of two concentrators. Because all the hosts connect
to the concentrators, the tool could easily deduce that polling the concentrators
is the correct behavior.

However, suppose you instructed the tool to produce billing information
for a region that has three hosts, two on a single concentrator and the third on
another. Now, the tool should be able to figure out that the correct approach is
to query each host individually for the necessary information.

Note that many networks contain redundant links, loops, and devices that
operate only when another device has a fault. These redundancies can make it
difficult for the tool to isolate which devices to query. If the tool encounters
any difficulty doing this, it should query you.

Once you have denoted a region of the network, the tool should ask for the following:

1. Information concerning how to bill (i.e., according to byte input, packet output, total connections, etc.)
2. Pricing information for the region (i.e., cost per byte)
3. How often to poll for data (i.e., hourly, daily, etc.)

At this point the billing process for the region would begin, that is, the billing data would be gathered and placed into the relational database. This billing process is illustrated in Flowchart 6.1.

AN ADVANCED TOOL

The advanced tool should further enhance the accounting management capabilities by forecasting the need for network resources. This forecasting ability can help you establish reasonable metrics and quotas. Another feature of the advanced tool would help users predict their network billing costs.

Metric data and quotas can help you determine if network resources are sufficient. As with the simple tool, using the relational database allows the advanced tool to produce statistics that tell how often users have exceeded quotas over a specific time period. Extending this functionality, the advanced tool should be able to determine if a trend on the network is going to cause a quota to be reached and thus alert you to upgrade the resource, add more equipment to the resource, change the quota, or whatever other action you determine might be required.

For example, consider a private network within a company. Users employ a pool of modems to dial public machines to retrieve information. It would be reasonable for these users to have limits on the length of time they can use a modem. Let's say that when you first set up the modem pool, you had established an arbitrary time limit of 5 hours for a single call; at the end of 5 hours, the modems disconnect the call. For many years, this time limit has been adequate and has not prevented any transaction from being completed.

However, in the meantime, the company you work for entered into a joint development agreement with another organization. As part of this agreement, megabytes of information have had to be transferred between the two companies each night. At first, the transfers took only 3 hours. Now, though, as the development effort has expanded, more information needs to be sent across the connection, which means the transaction will now exceed the time limit for use of a single modem. However, because you had installed the advanced tool, the transfers are able to continue without disruption—the tool had noted that connection time was approaching the quota and informed you so you could

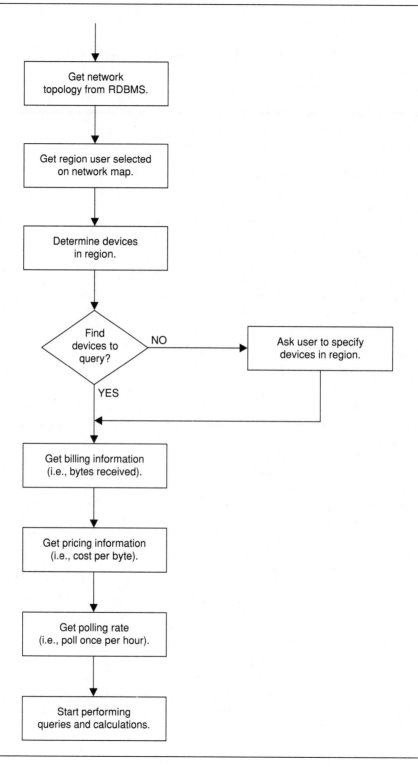

FLOWCHART 6.1 Flowchart for billing with the more complex tool.

change the quota. In this scenario, accounting management information led to a capacity redistribution decision.

The advanced tool also should be able to predict a network bill for users. To do this, the tool must be able to perform two steps: First, examine the relational database to determine any trend in bills for a particular user for past billing cycles and second, take all data available for the current billing cycle and extrapolate it to the end of a particular billing cycle.

To illustrate how the tool would do this, suppose the manager of a user group asks you for a prediction of the group's next network bill. You could input the data on the group into the tool, which would then search the billing information in the network management database and find all past records for the group. Suppose these records show an increase of five percent for each of the last 10 billing cycles. The tool next would check the information in the database for the current billing cycle. Extrapolating this information to the end of this cycle, the tool finds a six percent increase probable since the last billing cycle. This correlates closely to the five percent increases in the past. As output, the tool then would produce a bill for the requested billing cycle that includes a six percent increase over the last billing cycle.

However, suppose the extrapolation of information did not correlate closely to the past billing fees. This could happen either if the current billing cycle has just begun and the sample data is not reflective of a full billing cycle or the group has had an increase or decrease in network activity. In these cases, the tool would need to output a prediction based upon the historical data and then one derived from the current billing cycle.

6.4 Reporting Accounting Information

Accounting management information reports can be in the form of real-time messages and text reports. Real-time messages can inform you of the value of a certain metric while text reports can provide historical accounting and billing information.

For example, upon your request the network management system could bring up a real-time message window showing a metric for a device, as seen in Fig. 6.7. This message could show you the number of sessions being handled by the network device. This metric is important because the device performs protocol translation and only optimally can support a certain number of sessions.

The system also must generate text reports of accounting management statistics. These reports are similar to the output of the simple tool. Some are historical summaries of metrics; others can predict trends in the future usage of a network resource. You can use this information to plan realistic quotas for the network resources.

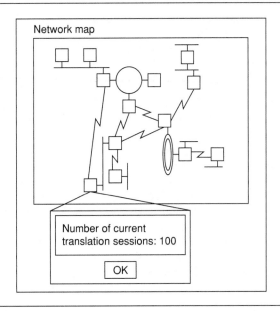

FIGURE 6.7
The screen of the network management system with a real-time accounting management message.

Also important are reports to give to each user about their network bill. These reports show the information used to derive the current bill and also predict the price of the next bill. Such a report might be similar to Table 6.3.

Summary

Accounting management enables the network engineer to measure the usage of network resources by users. Data obtained from these efforts are used to establish metrics, check and enforce quotas, determine costs, and bill users for their network usage.

This form of network management offers several benefits. By using the data obtained, the engineer can accurately bill each user to recover developmental and maintenance costs associated with the network. This data also can aid the engineer in allocating network resources more efficiently and in better understanding user utilization of those resources, thus creating a more productive network.

TABLE 6.3
NETWORK USAGE BILL: MARKETING GROUP

Billing period: November 1992 – December 1992
Number of total bytes received from network: 123 megabytes
Devices polled to determine above amount: MtkgHub1, MktgBridge

Price per megabyte:	$30.00
Current bill:	$3690.00
Bill last period:	$3240.00
Percent change:	14% INCREASE
Prediction for bill next period:	$4200.00
Prediction for percent change:	10% INCREASE

Accomplishing accounting management involves three steps: 1) gathering data about how users employ network resources, 2) using the data gathered to set and enforce usage quotas, and 3) billing users for their use of network resources.

As with the other forms of management we have discussed, how well the engineer can achieve accounting management depends on the level of tool available. We offered three different tools for your consideration.

A simple tool should be able to monitor for metrics that exceed quotas and report that data to you accordingly. It also should be able to store the metric data in the network management system relational database and calculate quotas employing a formula based on data from the database.

A more complex tool should go a step further and enable the engineer to perform network billing. It also could be able to determine itself where to poll for billing information. Finally, the advanced tool should further enhance accounting management effectiveness by forecasting the need for network resources, which can help the engineer establish reasonable metrics and quotas, and by helping users predict their network billing costs.

We also discussed methods for reporting accounting information and stressed the importance of using a real-time status display and text reports. Real-time messages keep the engineer informed about the current value of a metric; text reports provide valuable historical accounting and billing information.

For Further Study

Rhodes, P., *Lan Operations,* Addison-Wesley Publishing Company, Reading, Mass. 1991.

Terplan, K., *Communications Network Management, Second Edition,* Prentice-Hall, Englewood Cliffs, New Jersey, 1992.

7

Network Management Protocols

In this chapter:
- Definition of a network management protocol
- History of the network management protocols
- Development of standard protocols
- Introduction to
  - The MIB
  - ASN.1 Syntax
  - SNMP
  - CMIS/CMIP
  - CMOT
  - LMMP

As we saw in previous chapters, effective network management depends on the network engineer's being able to monitor and control the data network. Without this information, the engineer would be forced to make network management decisions without the benefit of adequate qualitative or quantitative measurements. Therefore it's essential they understand the methods available in the computing industry for monitoring and controlling the data network.

In this chapter, we introduce several network management protocols and review the development of this type of protocol. We also discuss the current methods available for getting and setting information on a data network, without which accomplishing the goals of network management would be impossible. With the help of the material presented in this chapter, network engineers should be better able to rate the various methods and determine which is suitable for their own data network.

7.1 History of Network Management Protocols

Until recently, gathering information from different network devices required engineers to learn a variety of methods by which to obtain the data. The reason for this is that as new networking products were developed, their manufacturers installed proprietary methods for enabling data collection from their products; the result was that two devices with the same functionality, but coming from different manufacturers, could provide vastly different methods for data collection.

For example, suppose a company uses two types of DECnet routers to connect Digital minicomputers. The first type is produced by a company called *RouteMe* and the second by a company named *FastRoute*. Both allow access via a remote login facility. However, the method you would use to actually access the data differs significantly. To ask a *RouteMe* router about the number of interfaces and operating parameters, you would use a menu driven system; to ask the *FastRoute* router for the same information, you would use three commands from a commandline interface. Figure 7.1 shows examples of these two different user interfaces.

As you can see, in a heterogeneous network environment, it can be slow and cumbersome to employ such diverse query methods. Network engineers needed a consistent method to gather information about all the components on the data network. Thus engineers turned to generic but standard tools. However, although these tools were simpler to use than the many methods provided by the manufacturers, they were not designed specifically for network management and so had their drawbacks, as discussed below.

On Internet Protocol (IP) data networks, network engineers can use the Internet Control Message Protocol (ICMP) Echo and Echo Reply messages to gather limited information useful for network management. Originally intended

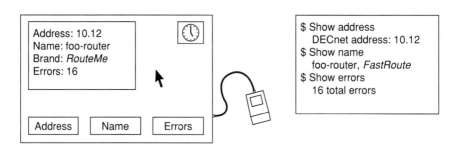

FIGURE 7.1
The same statistics displayed using a menu-driven interface and a commandline interface.

for sending control messages information between two network devices, most ICMP messages are not easily interpreted by humans. However, the tandem of ICMP Echo and Echo Reply messages, which exists on any device with the complete IP protocol suite, provides a quick method of checking the network connectivity to a remote device.

Using these messages, a host device on a network that receives an ICMP Echo must return an ICMP Echo Reply to the source host. A reply not received by the sending host can, but not always, indicate a lack of network connectivity between the two hosts. An application called *ping* (Packet InterNet Groper) tests network connectivity to a remote device by sending an ICMP Echo to the device and then waiting for the ICMP Echo Reply. Figure 7.2 shows the messages sent and received by a host using the ping application.

Most implementations of ping also can tell the overall turnaround time (usually in milliseconds) between the Echo message sent and the Echo Reply received, as well as the percentage of lost ICMP Reply messages between the source and destination. TCP/IP is not the only protocol suite with a tool like ping. The Echo/Echo Reply paradigm exists in several other protocols, such as Appletalk, Novell/IPX, Xerox XNS, and Banyan Vines. However, this model has the following drawbacks:

1. Unreliable delivery
2. Need for polling
3. Limited information

Most Echo/Echo Reply packets directly use the network layer, and are not guaranteed to be delivered by the transport layer. Thus, the failure of an Echo to travel between two locations does not always mean a lack of connectivity.

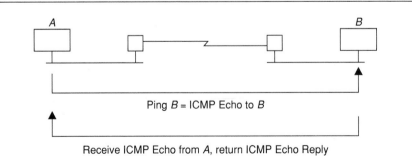

Ping *B* = ICMP Echo to *B*

Receive ICMP Echo from *A*, return ICMP Echo Reply

FIGURE 7.2
A uses ping to test network connectivity to *B*.

It might indicate that a network device dropped the Echo or Echo Reply because of a temporary lack of buffer space. Or, the packet might have failed because of congestion on a data circuit at the time of transmission.

To find out current information using Echo/Echo Reply you must continuously poll network devices. Performing this polling is a popular method of fault isolation, as it can be done quickly and easily and does not require any special privileges or additional hardware. A large percentage of lost Echo Replies could indicate a connectivity problem. However, this is the extent of the troubleshooting capability provided by this method. Once determined, the network engineer needs to rely on other methods to isolate and fix the problem. A protocol for network management should offer the ability to have devices send unsolicited messages to a management system. This may occur in addition to polling, but it is a more efficient method for gathering important network management information.

A primary reason for this deficiency is that Echo and Echo Reply messages were not written to provide a lot of information. Hence, the information yielded often is not enough on which to base firm network management decisions. For this purpose, you would be better off using a protocol written specifically for managing data networks and that would provide more of the necessary information. To be most useful to the engineer, this protocol also should work across a wide spectrum of network devices.

Because of these drawbacks, it became apparent within the industry that a standard system was urgently needed. Consequently, the networking community has been developing two divergent technologies designed specifically for network management. The first, the *Simple Network Management Protocol* (SNMP), so far has proved to be quite successful. The second, *Common Management Information Services/Common Management Information Protocol* (CMIS/CMIP), developed by the *International Organization for Standardization* (ISO),[1] is also beginning to impact the networking community. Both SNMP and CMIS/CMIP provide a means of obtaining information from or giving instructions to network devices, although neither offers direction in the actual use of the information gathered. Additionally, both these network management protocols conform to the ISO Reference Model for Open Systems Interconnection (OSI).[2] The ISO Reference Model is a 7-layer network architectural model developed by the ISO and CCITT[3] (International Telephone and Telegraph Consultative Committee).

---

[1]ISO is an international body that develops, suggests, and names standards for network protocols. A commonly known ISO achievement is the ISO Reference Model for OSI.

[2]OSI is a protocol suite for use on data networks.

[3]The CCITT is an international organization that defines standards and recommendations for the connection of telephone equipment.

7.2 Development of Standard Protocols

The examples and problems discussed in Section 7.1 don't do justice to the issues involved in managing a complex data network. It is unlikely that any data network would be built entirely from products provided by a single company. Eventually, the need could arise for networking products from many companies, such as hubs, bridges, routers, hosts, and so forth. Network engineers must plan for change and growth of the network.

Network management protocols recently have emerged to provide a uniform way of accessing any network device made by any manufacturer for a standard set of values. Queries for network devices may include the following:

1. The name of the device
2. The version of software in the device
3. The number of interfaces in the device
4. The number of packets per second on an interface of the device

Settable parameters for network devices may include the following:

1. The name of the device
2. The address of a network interface
3. The operational status of a network interface
4. The operational status of the device

Standardized network management protocols carry the additional benefit in that the data sent and returned by a device is of a uniform appearance.

Before going into any more detail about the main two standard network management protocols (SNMP and CMIS/CMIP) we have to take a quick detour into the background of how they developed and the players involved. The *Internet Activities Board* (IAB), which oversees the work in networking technology and protocols for the TCP/IP internetworking community, took on the task of coordinating work in selecting a standard network management protocol.

The IAB comprises two subgroups: the *Internet Engineering Task Force* (IETF) and the *Internet Research Task Force* (IRTF). The IETF is chartered to identify problems and coordinate problem solving in the areas of management, engineering, and operations of the Internet. The IRTF is responsible for researching problems concerning TCP/IP network community and the Internet.

Circa 1988, development was being pursued in three different network management protocol directions:

1. High-level Entity Management System (HEMS)
2. Simple Gateway Monitoring Protocol (SGMP)

3. Common Management Information Protocol (CMIP) over TCP

A small war ensued over which one the IAB would recommend. Request For Comments (RFC)[4] 1052 states the conclusions of the IAB about the future use of each protocol.

As a short-term solution, the IAB recommended the immediate implementation of a protocol called the Simple Network Management Protocol (SNMP), which was based on the Simple Gateway Monitoring Protocol (SGMP), for use as a common network management protocol with TCP/IP based networks. The IETF was responsible for the implementation of SNMP. The IAB emphasized that further development of SNMP should be aimed at keeping the protocol simple and focused on the areas of fault management and configuration management. At this time, however, SNMP is used by many organizations in all areas of network management.

For the long term, the IAB recommended the Internet research community explore CMIS/CMIP as the basis for a network management protocol to satisfy future requirements. CMIS/CMIP was developed by the ISO with different goals than the SNMP. SNMP was originally intended for use by IP devices only, while CMIS/CMIP was intended to be non-protocol specific and for use in the management of all network devices.

When the IAB evaluated CMIS/CMIP it considered an implementation of the protocol that uses TCP (Transmission Control Protocol) for transport. This combination of CMIS/CMIP over TCP became known as CMOT. Today, CMOT is no longer being considered as a protocol for wide use, as we will see in Section 7.6

The IAB and ISO are not the only organizations involved with the development of standard protocols. The CCITT and the IEEE[5] (Institute of Electrical and Electronic Engineers) also have worked toward the development of standard network management protocols, as we will see in Sections 7.5 and 7.6.

7.3 The Management Information Base

The *Management Information Base* (MIB) is a precise definition of the information accessible via a network management protocol. In RFC 1052, the IAB recommended high priority be placed on defining an extended MIB for use with SNMP

---

[4]RFC's are a numbered progression of papers that contain many ideas and concepts initiated by the networking community. Many RFC's have gone on to become network protocol standards.

[5]The IEEE is a professional organization that defines network standards.

and CMIS/CMIP, although this effort to make one MIB for both protocols might no longer be realistic.

Using a hierarchical, structured format, the MIB defines the network management information available from a device. Each device, to comply with the standard network management protocol, must use the format for displaying information that is defined by the MIB.

RFC 1065 describes the syntax and type of information available in the MIB for the management of TCP/IP networks. Entitled *Structure and Identification of Management Information for TCP/IP-based Internets* (SMI), this RFC defines simple rules for naming and creating types of information. Some of the types of information allowed by the SMI include a *Gauge,* an integer that may increase or decrease, and *TimeTicks,* which counts time in hundredths of seconds. RFC 1065 later was adopted by the IAB as a full standard in RFC 1155.

Using the rules of the SMI, RFC 1066 presented the first version of the MIB for use with the TCP/IP protocol suite. This standard, now known as MIB-I, explains and defines the exact information base needed for monitoring and controlling TCP/IP-based internets. RFC 1066 was accepted by the IAB as a full standard in RFC 1156.

RFC 1158 proposed a second MIB, MIB-II, for use with the TCP/IP protocol suite. This proposal, formalized as a standard and approved by the IAB in RFC 1213, extends the information base defined in MIB-I by expanding the set of objects defined in the MIB.

To facilitate the migration of vendor-specific protocols to a standard management protocol, RFC 1156 allows for expansion of the MIB for vendor-specific enhancements. For example, suppose a company wants to make the CPU utilization of their Ethernet bridge available via a network management protocol. MIB-II does not contain an object that corresponds to CPU utilization. However since vendor-specific enhancements within the MIB are allowed, the Ethernet bridge vendor can define a new object for CPU utilization. This ability to create new objects using the same standard SMI makes available information other than that in MIB-II. Several companies have extended MIB-II and developed vendor-specific MIBs that contain more objects than the MIB-II itself. Many vendor-specific MIBs exist today, as most network devices have software agents that support MIB-II and their own private extensions.

At the time of this writing, there is an effort within the networking community to produce MIBs that do not directly relate to TCP/IP environments. Each MIB would focus on a specific technology, such as FDDI, Token Ring, Ethernet, or bridging. This is a significant development because it would move the MIB from being a general source of data to defining information specific to a media type or device. Some of the proposed MIBs under development and their corresponding RFC number is summarized in Table 7.1.

TABLE 7.1

MIB Name	Proposed Standard
IEEE 802.5 Token Ring Interface Type MIB	RFC 1231
Remote Network Monitoring MIB (RMON)	RFC 1271
Ether-Like Interface Type MIB	RFC 1284
FDDI Interface Type MIB	RFC 1285
Bridge MIB	RFC 1286

ASN.1 SYNTAX

A subset of the ISO Abstract Syntax Notation One (ISO ASN.1) defines the syntax for the MIB. Each MIB uses the tree architecture defined in ASN.1 to organize all available information. Each piece of information in the tree is a *labeled node*. Each labeled node contains the following:

1. An object identifier
2. A short text description

The *object identifier* (OID) is a series of integers separated by periods that names the node and denotes the exact traversal of the ASN.1 tree. The *short text description* describes the labeled node.

A labeled node can have subtrees containing other labeled nodes. If the labeled node has no subtrees, or *leaf nodes,* it contains a value and is known as an *object*. Figure 7.3 shows a sample MIB tree with the corresponding ASN.1 numbers.

TRAVERSAL OF THE MIB TREE

The root node of the MIB tree doesn't have a name or number, but does have three subtrees, as follows:

1. ccitt (0), administered by the CCITT
2. iso (1), administered by the ISO
3. joint-iso-ccitt (2), jointly administered by ISO and CCITT

In addition, several other subtrees exist under the iso(1) node, including the ISO-defined subtree for other organizations, org(3). Under the org(3) subtree, a particular node of interest is the one used by the United States Department Of Defense (DOD): dod(6). All the information gathered from devices communicating via the DOD protocols such as TCP/IP resides in the subtree that has the complete object identifier of 1.3.6.1. This object identifier

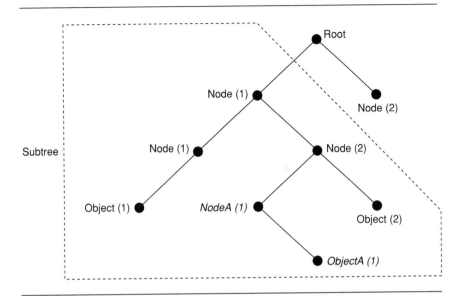

FIGURE 7.3
A sample ASN.1 tree. In this tree, *objectA* can be referenced by the OID as
1.2.1.1 or { *nodeA* 2 }.

is known as *internet*. The textual form for this identifier is { iso org(3) dod(6) 1 }.
Figure 7.4 shows the structure of the top of the MIB tree.

There are four defined subtrees under the internet object identifier, as follows:

1. directory (1)
2. mgmt (2)
3. experimental (3)
4. private (4)

In keeping with the accepted syntax, the short text description for the directory
node is { internet 1 }, the mgmt node is { internet 2 }, the experimental node
is { internet 3 }, and the private node is { internet 4 }.

Directory(1) Subtree.   Currently, the directory (1) subtree is reserved for
future use. It is foreseen that this subtree will contain information about the
OSI directory service (X.500).

Mgmt(2) Subtree.   The mgmt (2) subtree is intended for the assignment of
management information for DOD protocols. At the time of this writing, the
objects in this subtree are the most widely implemented. MIB-I (RFC 1156)

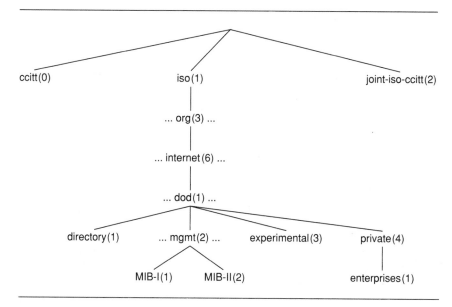

FIGURE 7.4
The ASN.1 tree used for network management.

has been assigned the object identifier 1.3.6.1.2.1 or { mgmt 1 } and MIB-II (RFC 1213) has been assigned 1.3.6.1.2.2 or { mgmt 2 }.

Beneath the mgmt(2) subtree are the objects used to obtain specific information from the network devices. These objects are broken down into 11 categories, which we list in Table 7.2 along with the types of information found in each category.

TABLE 7.2

10 Categories of Mgmt (2) Subtree	Information in the Category
system (1)	network device operating system
interfaces (2)	network interface specific
address translation (3)	address mappings
ip (4)	Internet Protocol specific
tcp (6)	Transmission Protocol specific
udp (7)	User Datagram Protocol specific
egp (8)	Exterior Gateway Protocol specific
cmot (9)	Common Management Information Services on TCP specific
transmission (10)	transmission protocol specific
snmp (11)	SNMP specific

The address translation(3) category maps IP addresses to Ethernet addresses. However, the MIB is intended to specify management information for protocols other than IP (such as the OSI network protocols). RFC 1213 removed this category in favor of letting the translation occur in each protocol-specific subtree. The cmot(9) category, discussed in Section 7.6, exists only for historical reasons.

Figure 7.5 shows the structure of the mgmt (2) subtree and includes some of the objects within each category.

Experimental (3) Subtree.   Experimental protocols and MIB development intended to enter the standards track use the third subtree, experimental (3). All objects that fall under this DOD subtree have object identifiers that begin with the integer 1.3.6.1.2.3. An experimental new MIB might be assigned the number 10 which correlates to the object identifier { experimental 10 }.

Private (4) Subtree.   The private(4) subtree is used to specify objects defined unilaterally. The most accessed portion of this subtree for many network

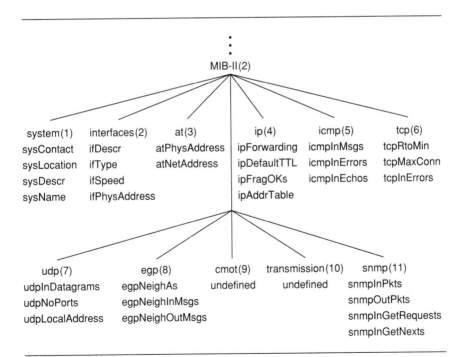

FIGURE 7.5
The various categories and some objects in MIB-II.

management systems is the enterprises(1) or { private 1 } node. An enterprise is an organization that has registered its own specific extensions to the MIB. Each subtree under this node is assigned to a single enterprise. The enterprise then can create attributes under this subtree specific to its products. Vendor-specific MIBs are found at this location in the hierarchy.

For example, if a company named Zeus received the subtree designation of 22, its object identifier representation would be 1.3.6.1.4.22 or { enterprises 22 }. A product of the Zeus company, such as its new multi-port translational bridge, might have the object identifier 1.3.6.1.4.22.1.

7.4 SNMP

Currently, the network management protocol most in use for data networks is the Simple Network Management Protocol (SNMP). RFC 1067 first defined how information passed between network management systems and agents with SNMP. RFC 1098 later made RFC 1067 obsolete. Then, with RFC 1157, the IAB accepted the proposal of RFC 1098 and in doing so, recognized SNMP as a standard protocol. Table 7.3 summarizes the RFC numbers for the history of SNMP.

RFC 1157 describes the agent/station model used in SNMP. An *SNMP agent* is software capable of answering valid queries from an *SNMP station,* such as a network management system, about information defined in the MIB. A network device that provides information about the MIB to the station will have an SNMP agent. For the agent/station model to work, the agent and station must speak the same language. Figure 7.6 shows the relationship between an SNMP agent and a station.

GETTING INFORMATION WITH SNMP

The SNMP agents and stations communicate through standard messages. Each of these messages are single packet exchanges. Because of this, SNMP uses UDP

TABLE 7.3

Description	Proposal RFC	Standard RFC
IAB Recommendations	–	1052
SNMP	1067/1098	1157
SMI	1065	1155
MIB-I	1066	1156
MIB-II	1158	1231

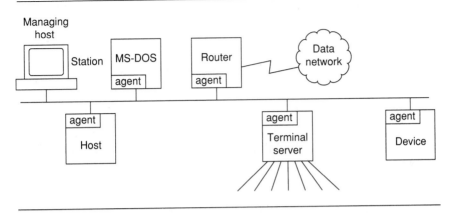

FIGURE 7.6
An SNMP station queries the SNMP agent present in network devices.

(User Datagram Protocol) as the layer 4, or transport layer, protocol. UDP uses a connectionless service, so SNMP does not have to maintain a connection between an agent and station to transmit a message. Figure 7.7 shows the ISO Reference Model for SNMP.

Layer 7	SNMP
Layer 6	ISO presentation
Layer 5	ISO session
Layer 4	UDP
Layer 3	IP
Layer 2	ISO data link
Layer 1	Physical

FIGURE 7.7
SNMP in the ISO reference model.

SNMP has five valid types of messages:

1. Get-Request
2. Get-Response
3. Get-Next-Request
4. Set-Request
5. Trap

The SNMP station uses Get-Request to retrieve information from a network device that has an SNMP agent. The SNMP agent in turn responds to the Get-Request message with a Get-Response message. Information that might be exchanged includes the name of the system, how long the system has been running, and the number of network interfaces on the system.

Get-Request and Get-Next-Request used in conjunction obtain a table of objects. Get-Request retrieves one specific object; Get-Next-Request then is used to ask for the next object in the table.

For example, you can use the network management system to determine the status of each interface on a device. The system could have the station send a Get-Request message to the agent on the device and ask for the single object that tells the number of interfaces:

```
{ iso org(3) dod(6) internet(1) mgmt(2) mib(1) inter-
faces(2) ifNumber(1) }.
```

Once the number of interfaces is determined, the network management system then could query the table about the information for each interface,

```
{ iso org(3) dod(6) internet(1) mgmt(2) mib(1) inter-
faces(2) ifTable(2) },
```

starting with the Get-Request command for the first interface. For each additional interface, the information is retrieved using Get-Next-Request. Figure 7.8 shows the sequence of Get-Request and Get-Next-Request messages used for this process.

Set-Request allows for the remote configuration of parameters on a device. Examples of Set-Request messages include setting the name of a device, shutting an interface administratively down, or clearing an address resolution table entry. In our example above, the network management system used Get-Request and Get-Next-Request to determine the number of interfaces on a particular device. Let's say that when the system examines the status of each interface, it discovers that one of the interfaces is not operational. By comparing the device parameters with an internal table, the system learns that the dysfunctional interface has the incorrect address. It then could use Set-Request to change the address of the interface in an attempt to bring it into an operational state.

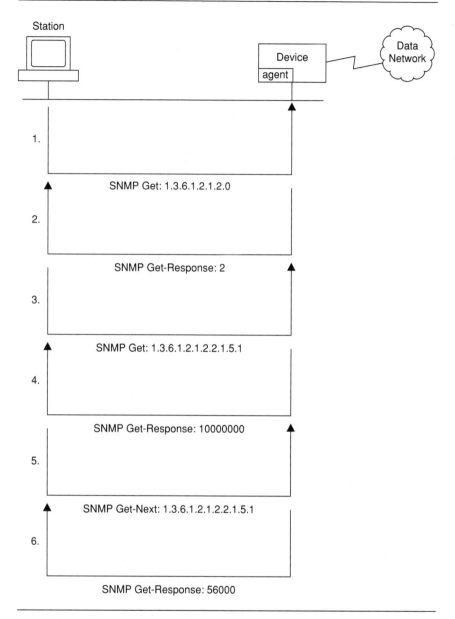

Station

Device
agent

Data
Network

1.

SNMP Get: 1.3.6.1.2.1.2.0

2.

SNMP Get-Response: 2

3.

SNMP Get: 1.3.6.1.2.1.2.2.1.5.1

4.

SNMP Get-Response: 10000000

5.

SNMP Get-Next: 1.3.6.1.2.1.2.2.1.5.1

6.

SNMP Get-Response: 56000

FIGURE 7.8
Using SNMP to determine the speed of all interfaces on a device.

1. Get the total number of interfaces from the device.
2. Reply is two interfaces.
3. Get the first entry in the table, return the speed of the interface.
4. Reply is 10000000 bps.
5. Get the next entry in the table, return the speed of the interface.
6. Reply is 56000 bps.

SNMP Trap.   An SNMP Trap is an unsolicited message an SNMP agent sends
to a station. These messages inform the server about the occurrence of a
specific event. For example, SNMP Trap messages can be used to inform
the network management system that a circuit has just failed, the disk space
of a device is nearing capacity, or a user has just logged onto a host. Figure
7.9 shows the interaction between the SNMP station and an agent in a device
sending a SNMP Trap.

Currently, seven types of SNMP Traps are defined as part of MIB-II, as follows:

1. Coldstart of a system
2. Warmstart of a system
3. Link down
4. Link up
5. Failure of authentication
6. Exterior Gateway Protocol (EGP) neighbor loss
7. Enterprise-specific

The *coldstart trap* indicates that the agent sending the trap is reinitializing
itself such that its configuration or protocol implementation has changed. A
coldstart trap occurs when a device is powered on. The *warmstart trap* indicates
that the device sending the trap is reinitializing itself such that its configuration
or protocol implementation has not changed. If the SNMP agent in a device is
reset, this action would invoke a warmstart trap. Typically, this event occurs
because of manual intervention.

A *link down trap* means a specific link on the source device has failed; a
link up trap signifies a specific link from the source device has come up.

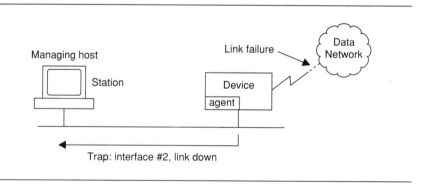

FIGURE 7.9
After receiving an SNMP trap, the management host can immediately inform
the network engineer about a specific network event.

A *failure of authentication trap* message is sent to the network management system if an SNMP agent determines that a request does not provide proper authentication, for instance, if the agent gives the wrong SNMP community string. (We explain SNMP community strings later in this section.) This information can lead to the implementation of security management.

An *Exterior Gateway Protocol (EGP) neighbor loss trap* is used by an SNMP agent to report the loss of an EGP neighbor. EGP is a reachability protocol used between data networks.

Enterprise-specific traps outnumber the generic traps by many orders of magnitude. Some companies have implemented traps based on disk usage on a workstation. Various network devices can send traps based upon high utilization or error rates found on network links. There are unlimited numbers of potential enterprise-specific SNMP Traps that can be implemented by vendors on their specific network devices.

Community Strings. The SNMP protocol does not provide information or allow configuration changes of a network device without some form of security. The SNMP agent in the network device can require that the SNMP station send a particular password with each message. The SNMP agent then would verify if the station is authorized to access MIB information. This password is referred to as the SNMP *community string*. Figure 7.10 shows how an SNMP agent reacts to receiving valid and invalid community strings.

Some implementations of SNMP agents allow for different levels of security using the community string. For example, the agent could define a community string to allow Get-Request and Get-Next-Request messages from a set of stations; these stations would have a read-only access to the information in the MIB. Or, the agent could allow Get-Request, Get-Next-Request, and Set-Request messages from another set of stations; these stations would have full (read-write) access to the agent.

Community strings are sent within SNMP packets in clear ASCII text. With little effort, a network literate person can learn the community string used by a given SNMP agent. Because this easy access presents a potential security problem, enhancement of the security feature of SNMP is currently receiving considerable attention. At the time of this writing, the IETF has a working group tasked with specifying security services for SNMP.

PROBLEMS WITH SNMP

Although SNMP is a powerful protocol for network management, it currently has two drawbacks:

1. It is officially only standardized for use on IP networks, and
2. it is inefficient for large table retrievals.

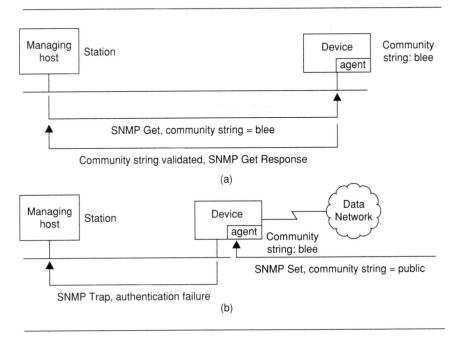

FIGURE 7.10
(a) An SNMP query with a valid community string. (b) An SNMP query with an invalid community string.

First, the RFC standard only defines the implementation of SNMP on IP networks. IP is a widespread datagram protocol and can be found on almost any computer today. However, not all networks rely on IP for delivery. This is one reason why some in the networking community recognize SNMP as a temporary solution to the need for a standard network management protocol.

A possible solution to this problem are the use of SNMP Proxy agents. *SNMP Proxy agents* can gather information from network devices that don't speak IP and then convey this information to a management station with SNMP, thus allowing non-IP network devices to be managed via SNMP. A disadvantage of SNMP Proxy agents is that specific software must be written for each network device.

Another possible solution is to implement SNMP on top of other transport protocols, thus allowing it to work in networks that do not support IP. The definition of SNMP over OSI does exist[6], but to date remains unimplemented.

[6]Specified in RFC 1161.

Companies such as Novell, Inc. and Apple Computer, Inc. have recently announced they will soon support SNMP on top of their proprietary protocols.

Another problem with using SNMP is that SNMP can be inefficient in retrieving large tables of data. As described earlier in this section, retrieval of tables with SNMP is accomplished with Get-Next-Request messages. However, using this message to retrieve large tables of data can burden both the network and the destination SNMP agent. For example, suppose you wanted to get a 2000-entry accounting table from a device. Each row in the accounting table has four entries: a source address, a destination address, a byte count, and a packet count. Using Get-Next-Request messages, in the best case (no retransmissions), you would end up with 2 x 4 x 2000, or 16,000 packets. This product is derived by multiplying four requests per row by 2000 rows and multiplying that product by the number of associated Get-Request and Get-Response messages. If the station requested all four items for each row in a single packet, the total would be 2 x 2000, or 4000 packets on the data network. Even with this significant reduction of traffic, the SNMP agent on the destination device still must perform 16,000 lookups in the accounting table.

One company, Cisco Systems, Inc. of Menlo Park, California, has recently developed a possible solution to this problem. The SNMP agent in the Cisco Systems devices works over both TCP and UDP. Cisco defined a new SNMP message, called Get-Column, that allows for the efficient retrieval of a column of data from a table of information via SNMP using TCP.

Get-Column works by having the station request an entire column from a table in one packet. Doing this results in many Get-Response messages from a single Get-Column message, the same amount as seen above when we used Get-Next-Request messages. This action also might result in as many agent lookups, depending on the implementation. But because Get-Column uses TCP for transport, it provides for a more reliable data transfer and better handling of network congestion. This also means that the SNMP agent and station must maintain a connection for the duration of a Get-Column transaction. The use of TCP results in a more complex protocol that requires resources for a connection on both the station and the agent, but Get-Column does appear to be one solution to reliably transferring large amounts of data with SNMP. Currently, this Get-Column Request is proprietary, so this solution is only available on Cisco Systems, Inc. devices.

7.5 CMIS/CMIP

Many people feel that the protocol suite that may be best able to satisfy network management needs is the OSI network management protocol Common Management Information Services/Common Management Information Protocol (CMIS/CMIP).

CMIS defines the services provided by each network component for network management. These services are general, not specific in nature. CMIP is the protocol that implements the CMIS services.

OSI network protocols are intended to provide a common network architecture for all devices on each layer of the ISO Reference Model. In the same manner, CMIS/CMIP intends to provide a complete network management protocol suite for use with any network device.

To provide the needed network management protocol features over many, diverse network machines and computer architectures, the functionality and structure of CMIS/CMIP is significantly different from that of SNMP. SNMP was designed for simplicity and ease of implementation. The OSI network management protocols are not as simplistic as SNMP, but they can provide the functionality needed to support a total network management solution.

To deal with CMIS/CMIP, you first need to understand the terminology of OSI as it relates to network management. A system, whether it is a network component such as a source route bridge or a workstation using the OSI protocol stack, is referred to as *an open system*. Two devices that communicate using the OSI protocols at the same ISO Reference Model layer are *peer open systems*.

The entire structure of the OSI network management protocols assumes the ISO Reference Model is being used. Network management application processes use the application layer of the ISO Reference Model. Also in this layer, the Common Management Information Service Element (CMISE)[7] provides the means for applications for using CMIP. Included in this seventh layer are two more ISO application protocols: (1) Association Control Service Element (ACSE)[8] and (2) Remote Operations Service Element (ROSE)[9]. Figure 7.11 shows the CMIP protocols in the ISO Reference Model for CMIS. Note that ACSE establishes and closes associations between applications; ROSE handles request/reply interactions between applications.

These protocols, and the applications that use them, comprise the framework for the ISO network management scheme. Other than those protocols defined on the application layer, OSI does not define protocols on the lower layers specifically for network management.

GETTING INFORMATION WITH CMIS

CMIS services provide the basic building blocks and intrinsic functionality for a system as it works to solve the puzzle of systems management. Any application that performs systems management is a *CMISE-service-user*. The existence of

---

[7]Specified in ISO 9595/9596.
[8]Specified in ISO 8649/8650.
[9]Specified in ISO DIS 9072-1/2.

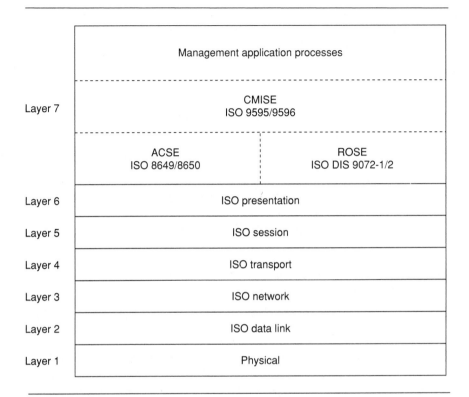

FIGURE 7.11
The CMIP protocols in the ISO Reference Model.

defined services for interaction between peer open systems is an important difference between CMIS and SNMP. CMIS has defined three classes of services, as follow:

1. Management association
2. Management notification
3. Management operation

Management Association Services. The first class of service, *management association service*, controls the association between peer open systems. These services are used primarily for the establishment and release of connections between systems. They control the initialization, termination, and abnormal release of a connection of a management association with the following services:

1. M-INITIALIZE
2. M-TERMINATE
3. M-ABORT

The M-INITIALIZE service institutes an association with a peer CMISE-service-user for systems management. The M-TERMINATE service terminates a connection between peer CMISE-service-users. The M-ABORT service is used when a connection between CMISE-service-users terminates in an abnormal manner.

These management association services each assume the use of services of ACSE for operation. Other CMIS services operate with ROSE. According to the ISO model, both ACSE and ROSE assume the use of the ISO presentation service and the remainder of the ISO Reference Model.

Management Notification Services.   The second type of service CMIS provides is *management notification.* In the same manner that SNMP Trap messages provide information about events on a network, management notification services provide similar functionality for CMIS. The M-EVENT-REPORT service tells a peer CMISE-service-user about an event that has occurred on another CMISE-service-user. If the CMISE-service-user on a system notes the change of a value (such as the state change of an interface), it can notify the managing system with the M-EVENT-REPORT service. Unlike with the SNMP Trap service, however, these events are not strictly defined. Rather, they are specific to the system that generated the notification.

Management Operation Services.   The *management operation services* comprise the third group as follows:

1. M-GET
2. M-SET
3. M-ACTION
4. M-CREATE
5. M-DELETE

The M-GET service is used by a CMISE-service-user to retrieve management information from a peer CMISE-service user. It is analogous to the SNMP Get-Request message.

The CMIS M-SET service allows a CMISE-service-user to modify the management information of a peer CMISE-service-user. This service is similar to the SNMP Set-Request message that allows modification of information on a network device.

The M-ACTION service is invoked by a CMISE-service-user to instruct a peer CMISE-service-user to perform a desired action. The actions performed are relative to each specific device. For example, an open system request could request a peer to send ICMP Echoes (pings) to various locations to test IP network connectivity. There are many actions that an open system can request another open system to perform. Figure 7.12 shows one use of the M-ACTION service.

The M-CREATE service is used by a CMISE-service-user to instruct a peer CMISE-service-user to create another instance of a managed object. The managed object represents the CMISE-service-user on the managed system. In CMIS, each object that is managed has an associated instance. CMIS allows many instances of the same object, but only one definition of the object itself. This is similar in concept to object oriented programming, where each object has a definition called a *class* and each use of this definition is called an *instance of the class*. One way to use the M-CREATE service is to allow managed objects to instruct each other about the presence of new objects. For example, on a management system, there might exist a definition of a Ethernet bridge. Each time a new bridge is added, the management system would create and use an instance of this definition.

The last of the management operation services is M-DELETE. The converse of M-CREATE, this service is used by a CMISE-service-user to ask that a peer delete an instance of a managed object.

In the same way that SNMP uses community strings to verify that a system can access the management information, CMIS uses access lists. For each open

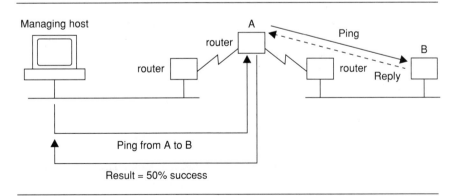

FIGURE 7.12
A typical M-ACTION service.

system, these access lists explicitly state the access of other open systems. At the time of this writing, the access control remains in an unspecified form. It is intended, however, that a CMISE-service-user would check the access control before the invocation of any CMIS service.

Management Associations.   A *management association* is the connection between two peer open systems for systems management. The process of connection relies on CMISE to interface with other protocols on the OSI protocol stack. With CMIS, four possible types of associations can exist between peer open systems, as follows:

1. Event
2. Event/Monitor
3. Monitor/Control
4. Full Manager/Agent

An Event association permits two open systems to send M-EVENT-RE-PORT messages. The Event/Monitor association is the same as the Event association except that each system also may receive and issue M-GET messages. The Monitor/Control association allows for the communication of M-GET, M-SET, M-CREATE, M-DELETE, and M-ACTION requests, although no event reporting is allowed. The Full Manager/Agent association supports all of the CMIS services.

CMIP.   The missing piece in our discussion of the OSI network management protocols deals with the implementation of the concepts set out by CMIS. The protocol that implements CMIS is the Common Management Information Protocol (CMIP). The specification of this protocol explains in detail the manner in which the protocol should perform for each of the CMIS services.

The CMIP protocol requires a CMIP machine, or a CMIPM, to function according to a defined specification. A *CMIPM* is software that performs two functions: First, it accepts operations sent to it by a CMISE-service-user through the CMIS services and initiates the appropriate procedure to accomplish the associated operation. Second, CMIPM sends valid CMIP messages, in the form of a CMIS service request, received from the network to the CMISE-service-user.

Important to the definition of CMIP is that CMIP only defines how to decipher the information in a packet; it does not state what a CMISE-service-user should do with any information requested from a managed object. Thus the CMIP specifications don't infringe at all on the functionality of the network management system. The network management system can request any relevant information from a managed object and interpret that information in any manner.

PROBLEMS WITH CMIS/CMIP

The protocol suite of CMIS/CMIP provides the networking community with a management protocol capable of performing many tasks. There are, however, two critical problems with the CMIS/CMIP suite, as follows:

1. It requires a large amount of overhead.
2. It is difficult to implement.

Although the two problems above are listed separately, they result directly from the fact that CMIS/CMIP is designed to run on a fully implemented OSI protocol stack. Because of the full-featured nature of the OSI protocols, they provide flexible functionality and use vast amounts of overhead. Some network devices may not have the memory or processing power to support the full OSI stack. For some vendors this makes the OSI stack difficult to implement because of hardware or software restrictions. There are many implementations of the OSI stack, but at this time they are not widely deployed.

7.6 CMOT

The *Common Management Information Services and Protocol over TCP/IP* (CMOT) proposes to implement the CMIS services on top of the TCP/IP protocol suite. Doing this is meant to be an interim solution until extensive deployment of the OSI protocol stack solution. RFC 1189 defines the CMOT protocol. Figure 7.13 shows the CMOT protocols on the ISO Reference Model.

The application protocols used by CMIS don't change with the implementation of CMOT. CMOT relies on the protocols CMISE, ACSE, and ROSE, as previously described with CMIS. However, instead of waiting for the implementation of the ISO Presentation Layer protocol, CMOT requires the use of another protocol on the same layer of the ISO Reference Model—the *Lightweight Presentation Protocol* (LPP), as defined in RFC 1085. This protocol provides the interface to either of the two most common Transport Layer protocols used today—UDP and TCP, which both use IP for network delivery.

A system that complies with the CMOT specification must have the functionality to establish one of the recognized associations—that is, Event, Event/Monitor, Monitor/Control, or Full Manager/Agent—with an open system. This system also must support only the type of association that is appropriate to the system. For example, it might not make sense for the software controlling a modem rack to implement an entire Full Manager/Agent association. However, it could be appropriate for the software to report events with an M-EVENT-REPORT message and to answer queries from an M-GET message. Possibly this system would implement only the Event/Monitor association. On

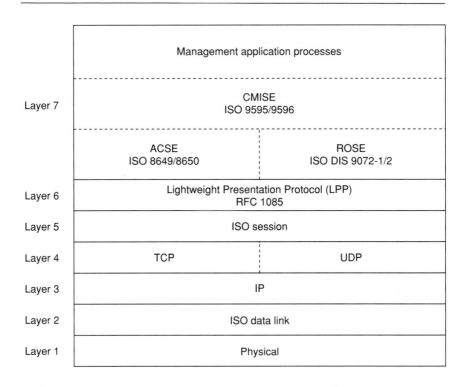

FIGURE 7.13
The CMOT protocols in the ISO Reference Model.

the other hand, it's feasible to assume that a complete network management system would implement the Full Manager/Agent association.

A potential problem with using CMOT is that many network management vendors don't want to spend time implementing another interim solution. Time spent working on a short-term solution is seen as less than ideal. Instead, numerous vendors have jumped on the SNMP bandwagon and spent considerable resources in this effort. In fact, although the definition for CMOT exists, no significant work has been done on the protocol for quite some time.

7.7 LMMP

The IEEE 802.1b *LAN Man Management Protocol* (LMMP) attempts to provide a network management solution for LAN environments. LMMP was formerly known as Common Management Information Services and Protocol over IEEE

802 Logical Link Control (CMOL). Examples of network devices within a LAN environment include transparent and source route bridges, wiring hubs, and repeaters. This protocol, developed recently by 3Com Corp. and IBM, eliminates the need for the OSI protocols to implement the CMIS services. Because LMMP rides directly on top of IEEE 802 Logical Link Layer (LLC), it does not rely on any specific network layer protocol, such as IP, for network delivery.

By not requiring any network layer protocol, LMMP is potentially easier to implement than CMIS/CMIP or CMOT. Yet without a network layer to provide routing information, LMMP messages cannot traverse routers. However, the implementation of proxy agents to convey the LMMP information beyond the boundaries of a local area network might overcome this problem.

Summary

Before the existence of standard network management protocols, network engineers had to learn many methods for monitoring and controlling network devices. These methods could involve using a menu driven system or memorizing specific commands for a network device. The networking community then turned to generic methods, such as ping on TCP/IP networks, to help gather information for network management. However, these solutions lacked functionality and the ability to get the needed data.

The need for a method that worked on many devices prompted the development of standard protocols. Three network management protocols were examined, each of which strived, in a generic manner, to solve the problems associated with network management. After investigating these protocols, the IAB set forth a plan for the development of network management. RFC's document this plan and the associated standards.

Specified in the RFC's, the SMI defines how the information is structured and the MIB defines what information can be managed with the network management protocols. The MIB uses ASN.1 syntax.

SNMP was the first network management protocol in wide use. SNMP agents and stations communicate through a common protocol to get and set management information on data networks. However, SNMP by definition is to be implemented over TCP/IP-based internets, although there are proprietary protocol implementations as well.

The OSI network management protocol suite, CMIS/CMIP, provides the functionality that might be necessary for a complete network management solution. However, CMIS/CMIP relies on the implementation of the entire OSI protocol suite, which currently is not widely deployed.

As an interim solution, CMOT provides the functionality of CMIS on the TCP/IP protocol stack. The main drawback to CMOT is that many vendors don't want to spend time implementing an interim solution network management protocol. Currently, there is no work being done on CMOT.

Instead of producing another interim network management protocol, IBM and 3Com have proposed LMMP, which incorporates the CMIS services directly on the IEEE 802 Logical Link Layer. By virtue of its definition, LMMP messages are limited to a single local area network segment.

For Further Study

Case, J., M. Fedor, M. Schoffstall, and C. Davin, RFC 1157, *Simple Network Management Protocol (SNMP)*, May 1990.

Comer, D., *Internetworking With TCP/IP*, Volume I, Prentice-Hall, Englewood Cliffs, New Jersey, 1991.

International Organization For Standardization, Open Systems Interconnection, *Specification of Basic Specification of Abstract Syntax Notation One (ASN.1)*, International Standard Number 8824, ISO, Switzerland, May 1987b.

International Organization For Standardization, Open Systems Interconnection, *Specification of Basic Encoding Rules for Abstract Syntax Notation One (ASN.1)*, International Standard Number 8825, ISO, Switzerland, May 1987b.

International Organization For Standardization, Open Systems Interconnection, *Management Information Service Definition, Part 2: Common Management Information Service*, International Draft International Standard Number 9595-2, ISO, Switzerland, May 1988a.

International Organization For Standardization, Open Systems Interconnection, *Management Information Protocol Definition, Part 2: Common Management Information Protocol*, International Draft International Standard Number 9596-2, ISO, Switzerland, May 1988a.

McCloghrie, K., and M. Rose, RFC 1156, *Management Information Base for network management information of TCP/IP-based internets*, May 1990.

McCloghrie, K., and M. Rose, RFC 1213, *Management Information Base for network management information of TCP/IP-based internets:MIBII*, March 1991.

Rose, M., and K. McCloghrie, RFC 1155, *Structure and identification of management information for TCP/IP-based internets*, May 1990.

Rose, M., *The Simple Book: An Introduction to Management of TCP/IP-based Internets*, Prentice-Hall, Englewood Cliffs, New Jersey, 1991.

Rose, M., *The Open Book: A Practical Perspective on OSI*, Prentice-Hall, Englewood Cliffs, New Jersey, 1990.

Satz, G., *A New View on Bulk Retrieval with SNMP*, The Simple Times, Volume 1, Number 1, March/April 1992.

8

A Look at RFC 1213

In this chapter:
- Using RFC 1213
- Using MIB objects

In this chapter, we examine each section of RFC 1213, the *Management Information Base for Network Management of TCP/IP-based internets: MIB-II*. In this book, we refer to it as the "MIB." Our purpose in discussing the MIB is to help network engineers and developers of network management applications decide how to use the information in it. First, we define certain basic terms applicable to the MIB. Then, in the next eleven sections, we deal with various subtrees of the MIB. Included in this treatment is a discussion of *MIB objects*—that is, specific information accessible by the SNMP agent on a network device or computer system—and how to use these objects in network management. For each MIB group, we list the objects that apply to the various types of network management. Although space restraints prevent our discussing all of these objects as they apply to network management, we do examine as many as feasible. All functions described in this chapter can be performed by the network engineer manually or, preferably, by the appropriate network management application. We take the approach that the application, rather than the engineer, performs the functions.

Many sections within the chapter reference RFC 1213; we recommend you have a copy of this document nearby when reading this material (see Appendix A for instructions on retrieving this RFC). Definitions and explanations of the syntax used with a MIB are available in RFC 1155, the *Structure and Identification of Management Information for TCP/IP-based internets (SMI)*. This MIB also contains information pertaining to many protocols in the TCP/IP suite[1]. Much of the discussion in this chapter assumes your prior knowledge of these protocols and how they work.

---

[1]A good reference on these protocols can be found in various Request For Comments (RFC). Many other sources for this information exist. Some are listed in *For Further Study* section of Chapter 1.

8.1 MIB Definitions

The first section of RFC 1213 defines the types of objects available in the MIB. This RFC imports object types as defined in RFC 1155 and RFC 1212, *Concise MIB Definitions*.

In the RFCs, a network device or computer system which has a SNMP agent is known as an *entity* and in this chapter, we use this term.

For this MIB, both of the object types *NetworkAddress* and *IpAddress* refer to an IP Address. Although the definition of NetworkAddress in RFC 1213 is generic and could pertain to any protocol, the MIB we discuss here applies only to IP entities.

A *Counter* is an object that is a nonnegative integer that increases until it reaches some maximum value, for example, the total number of errors received on an interface. In contrast, a *Gauge* is an object that is a nonnegative integer that can rise and fall, for example, the current number of packets in the output queue of an interface.

The *TimeTicks* object is a nonnegative integer that counts hundredths of a second since an event, for example, the amount of time a system has been operational.

RFC 1213 contains two new definitions, DisplayString and PhysAddress. A *DisplayString* specifies how to print ASCII strings. A *PhysAddress* defines how to format physical network addresses, such as Media Access Control (MAC) addresses.

8.2 The System Group

The *system group* contains data about the system in which the entity presides. Many of these objects are useful for fault management and configuration management.

SYSTEM GROUP OBJECTS FOR FAULT MANAGEMENT

The system group objects listed in Table 8.1 apply to fault management.

The object identifier found in sysObjectID classifies the vendor with the entity, helpful data when to solve a problem regarding a device requires you to know the device's manufacturer.

sysServices tells which level of the ISO Reference Model the device primarily services. The value returned is a sum of values for each layer using the formula $2^{(L-1)}$, where L is the protocol layer number. For example, a router that operates primarily at layer 3 would return a value of 4, $2^{(3-1)}$, while a host that runs transport layer services (layer 4) and application layer services

TABLE 8.1

Object	Information Useful for Fault Management
sysObjectID	The system manufacturer
sysServices	Which protocol layer the device services
sysUptime	How long the system has been operational

(layer 7) would return a value of 72, $2^{(7-1)} + 2^{(4-1)}$. This information is useful for debugging problems when the functionality of the device is unknown.

sysUptime tells how long a system has been functioning. A fault management application polling for this object can determine if the entity has restarted: If the application sees an monotonously increasing sysUptime, then the entity is known to be up; if the value of sysUptime is less than the previous value, then the entity has restarted since the last poll.

SYSTEM GROUP OBJECTS FOR CONFIGURATION MANAGEMENT

The system group objects in Table 8.2 pertain to configuration management.

For many entities, the software revision or operating system is available through sysDescr. This data can be useful both for managing the setup of the device and for troubleshooting. sysLocation, sysContact, and sysName tell you, respectively, the physical location of the system, a person to contact for problems, and the name of the network device, all of which is useful to know when you need to contact someone for physical access to a remote device.

8.3 The Interfaces Group

The *interfaces group* objects offer data about each specific interface on a network device and are useful in fault, configuration, performance, and accounting management.

The ifTable objects contain information about all the interfaces on an entity while an ifEntry is a row of information about a specific interface. The number of different ifEntry records is found in ifNumber; for example, if a device has three interfaces, the value of ifNumber would be 3 and there would be an array of three separate ifEntry records, one record for each specific interface. The object ifIndex is an integer that is an index of the array of ifEntry groups. The structure of the interfaces group is set out in Fig. 8.1.

TABLE 8.2

Object	Information Useful for Configuration Management
sysDescr	Description of the system
sysLocation	System's physical location
sysContact	Person responsible for the system
sysName	System's name

INTERFACES GROUP OBJECTS FOR FAULT MANAGEMENT

The interfaces group objects in Table 8.3 apply to fault management.

From ifAdminStatus and ifOperStatus combined, the fault management application can determine the current status of the interface. Both objects return integers: The number 1 means up, 2 down, and 3 testing. Table 8.4 summarizes the possible meanings of these objects with respect to a single interface.

We can interpret this table as follows:

- If both ifAdminStatus and ifOperStatus return up, the interface is operational.

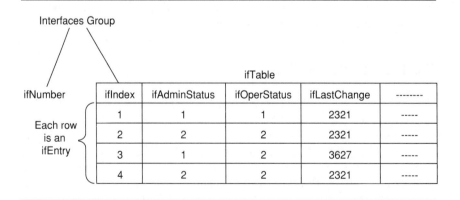

FIGURE 8.1
The interfaces group structure for a device with four interfaces. In this case, querying ifNumber would yield a value of 4. Note that in this figure, not all the objects available in each ifEntry are shown.

TABLE 8.3

Object	Information Useful for Fault Management
ifAdminStatus	Whether the interface is administratively up/down/test
ifOperStatus	Whether the interface operational state is up/down/test
ifLastChange	Time when the interface changed operational state

- If ifAdminStatus is up and ifOperStatus is down, the interface is in a failure mode.
- If both ifAdminStatus and ifOperStatus are down, the interface has been administratively turned off.
- If both ifAdminStatus and ifOperStatus return testing, the interface is in a testing mode (possibly loopback).

(All other combinations of the two objects are not applicable.)

If one of these four combinations is not returned by a query for ifAdminStatus and ifOperStatus, it could mean the entity or device software is working improperly. ifLastChange will contain the value of sysUpTime correlating to when the interface entered its current operational state.

INTERFACES GROUP OBJECTS FOR CONFIGURATION MANAGEMENT

The interfaces group objects in Table 8.5 apply to configuration management.

These objects give you information about the setup of an interface. ifDescr and ifType name the interface and give its type, respectively; for example, if ifDescr returned the string "Ethernet0", ifType might return the number 6. The meaning of the number returned by ifType is defined in the MIB. To be more helpful to you, one of the network management applications should map the

TABLE 8.4

| | ifAdminStatus | | |
	Up(1)	Down(2)	Testing(3)
ifOperStatus			
Up (1)	Operational	N/A	N/A
Down(2)	Failure	Down	N/A
Testing(3)	N/A	N/A	Testing

TABLE 8.5

Object	Information Useful for Configuration Management
ifDescr	Name of the interface
ifType	Type of interface
ifMtu	Maximum datagram through the interface
ifSpeed	Bandwidth of the interface
if AdminStatus	Whether the interface is administratively up/down/test

number 6 to a string that gives you more information about the interface type, such as "Ethernet-CSMA/CD".

ifSpeed is a Gauge that tracks the current interface speed in bits per second; for example, on an Ethernet interface ifSpeed typically returns 10000000, which represents 10 Mbps. This object is helpful for finding the current speed for an interface that may change, such as one that can allocate bandwidth on demand for heavy bursts of traffic.

ifAdminStatus tells you if an interface is administratively active. By sending a SNMP Set-Request you can use this object to remotely configure the interface on or off.

INTERFACES GROUP OBJECTS FOR PERFORMANCE MANAGEMENT

The interfaces group objects listed in Table 8.6 apply to performance management.

Performance management applications should be designed to watch the percentage of errors on an interface. To do this, the application must be able to find the total number of packets and errors on the interface. The application can determine the total number of packets received on the interface by totaling ifInUcastPkts and ifInNUcastPkts and the total number of packets sent on the interface by totaling ifOutUcastPkts and ifOutNUcastPkts. The percentages of input and output errors on the interface are found with the following equations:

$$\text{percent input errors} = \frac{\text{ifInError}}{(\text{ifInUcastPkts} + \text{ifInNUcastPkts})}$$

$$\text{percent output errors} = \frac{\text{ifOutErrors}}{(\text{ifOutUcastPkts} + \text{ifOutNUcastPkts})}$$

TABLE 8.6

Object	Information Useful for Performance Management
ifInDiscards	Rate of input discards
ifOutDiscards	Rate of output discards
ifInErrors	Rate of input errors
ifOutErrors	Rate of output error
ifInOctets	Rate of bytes received
ifOutOctets	Rate of bytes sent
IfInUcastPkts	Rate of input unicast packets
ifOutUcastPkts	Rate of output unicast packets
IfInNUcastPkts	Rate of input non-unicast packets
ifOutNUcastPkts	Rate of output non-unicast packets
ifInUnknownProtos	Rate of input unknown protocol packets
ifOutQLen	Total packets in the output queue

An application can use similar methods to monitor the number of packets discarded by the interface using the objects ifInDiscards and ifOutDiscards. Errors or discards can result from a variety of reasons: malfunctioning interface, media problems, buffering problems on the device, and so forth.

Once the errors have been discovered, you can set to work on resolving them. However, be aware that not all discards represent a problem. For example, a device may have a high percentage of discards because it's receiving many packets that are of an unknown protocol. The number of discards resulting from this situation is found in ifInUnknownProtos. Consider a network device that routes only the Internet Protocol. The device has an interface on an Ethernet where many personal computers form a network of clients and servers that send messages between themselves as Ethernet broadcasts. Because the network device has to pick up the broadcasts, it consequently receives many packets it does not know how to process, thus causing the number of ifInDiscards to climb and the number of ifInUnknownProtos to grow proportionally. As you can see, in this situation, a large number of ifInDiscards or ifInUnknownProtos may not indicate a problem.

A performance management application can use ifInOctets and ifOutOctets to compute the percent utilization on an interface. To perform this computation, two different polls would be required: one to find the total bytes at time x and another to find the total bytes at time y. The following equation computes total bytes sent and received between poll time x and y (x and y are in seconds):

$$\text{total bytes} = (\text{ifInOctets}_y - \text{ifInOctets}_x) + (\text{ifOutOctets}_y - \text{ifOutOctets}_x).$$

Next, calculate total bytes per second as follows:

total bytes per sec = total bytes/$(y - x)$.

Then line utilization is found as follows:

utilization = (total bytes per sec * 8)/ifSpeed.

In the equation for line utilization, the multiplication by 8 is necessary to convert from bytes to bits. The object ifSpeed is a number in bits per second.

Note, on an interface that operates at full duplex, such as a serial link, this equation will compute twice the interface utilization. For example, a serial link may operate at 64 Kbps in full duplex. Thus, if you totaled the input and output bytes of the interface, you then would be computing utilization for a 128 Kbps link. One possible solution to this problem is to compute as separate numbers the total bytes input and output over the given time period. Then, take the larger of these two numbers and divide by ifSpeed.

ifOutQLen tells whether a device is having trouble sending data out on the interface. The value of the object will increase as the number of packets waiting to leave the interface increases. Trouble sending data out could result from errors on the interface or the device's not being able to handle the packets as fast as they are input. While a large number of packets waiting in the output queue is not an immediate problem, its persistent growth might indicate congestion on the interface.

ifOutDiscards and ifOutOctets used together also may give an indication of network congestion. If a device is discarding many packets that are trying to leave the interface, as indicated by ifOutDiscards, and the total number of output bytes is decreasing, as shown by ifOutOctets, the interface might be congested.

INTERFACES GROUP OBJECTS FOR ACCOUNTING MANAGEMENT

The interfaces group objects shown in Table 8.7 apply to accounting management.

Using ifInOctets and ifOutOctets, an accounting management application can determine the number of bytes sent and received on an interface. This data can be helpful to the network device that has a direct interface to a single billing entity, a scenario we described in Chapter 6. If traffic traverses this interface in transit to another billing entity, the model doesn't work well. However, if the interface does connect to a single billing entity without transit traffic, no calculations are necessary to find out how many bytes the billing entity sent to or received from the network. If the billing model uses packet counts instead of bytes, ifInUcastPkts, ifOutUcastPkts, ifInNUcastPkts, and ifOutNUcastPkts give the data packet counts necessary to perform the billing process.

TABLE 8.7

Object	Information Useful for Accounting Management
ifInOctets	Total bytes received
ifOutOctets	Total bytes sent
IfInUcastPkts	Total unicast packets received
ifOutUcastPkts	Total unicast packets sent
IfInNUcastPkts	Total non-unicast packets received
ifOutNUcastPkts	Total non-unicast packets sent

8.4 The Address Translation Group

The address translation group is no longer a separate group. Its objects have been incorporated into other protocol groups and in this chapter, we examine the use of address translation information in network management as it appears in each of those groups.

8.5 The IP Group

The IP is a network protocol that uses a connection-less mode of service to deliver datagrams. The *IP group* provides information about the IP on the entity. This information is subdivided as follows:

1. Objects that give data about errors and the types of IP packets seen
2. A table of information about the IP addresses on this entity
3. IP routing table for the entity
4. The mapping of IP addresses to other protocol addresses. This section supercedes the features of the address translation group.

The structure of the IP group is shown in Fig. 8.2. These sections offer objects that can apply to fault, configuration, performance, and accounting management.

IP GROUP OBJECTS FOR FAULT MANAGEMENT

The IP group objects listed in Table 8.8 pertain to fault management.

All objects in the ipRouteTable can be useful for fault management; for example, for tracking routing problems and devices that advertise incorrect routing information. These objects enable the fault management application to produce the IP routing table for a device and discover routes through a network.

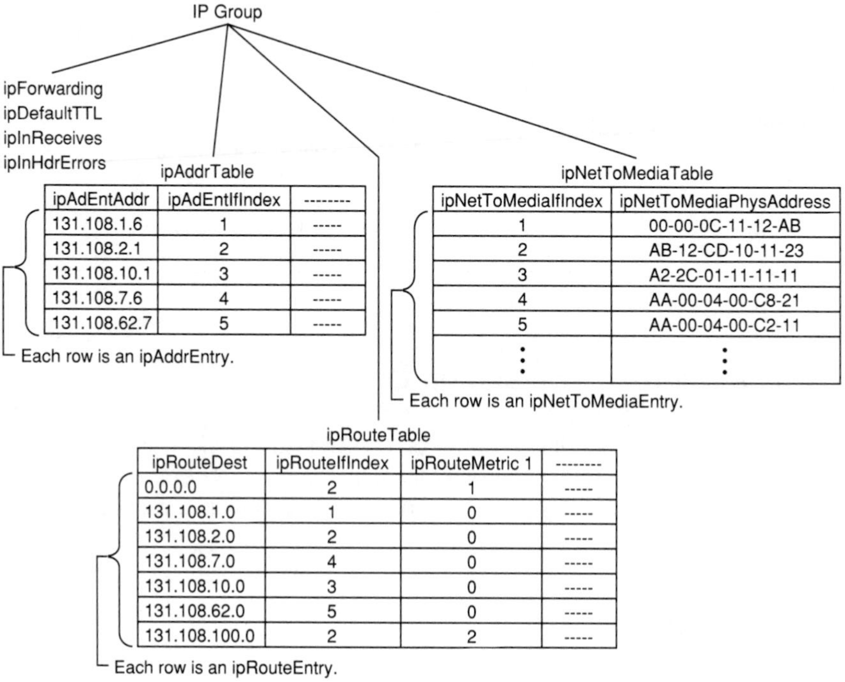

IP Group

ipForwarding
ipDefaultTTL
ipInReceives
ipInHdrErrors

ipAddrTable

ipAdEntAddr	ipAdEntIfIndex	--------
131.108.1.6	1	-----
131.108.2.1	2	-----
131.108.10.1	3	-----
131.108.7.6	4	-----
131.108.62.7	5	-----

Each row is an ipAddrEntry.

ipNetToMediaTable

ipNetToMediaIfIndex	ipNetToMediaPhysAddress
1	00-00-0C-11-12-AB
2	AB-12-CD-10-11-23
3	A2-2C-01-11-11-11
4	AA-00-04-00-C8-21
5	AA-00-04-00-C2-11
⋮	⋮

Each row is an ipNetToMediaEntry.

ipRouteTable

ipRouteDest	ipRouteIfIndex	ipRouteMetric 1	--------
0.0.0.0	2	1	-----
131.108.1.0	1	0	-----
131.108.2.0	2	0	-----
131.108.7.0	4	0	-----
131.108.10.0	3	0	-----
131.108.62.0	5	0	-----
131.108.100.0	2	2	-----

Each row is an ipRouteEntry.

FIGURE 8.2
The IP group is divided into four areas. Note that not all the objects for each table are shown.

Further, ipRouteType and ipRouteProto can tell how the routing information was learned.

Suppose for example a user cannot connect from *Kirk* to *Spock*. The network setup for this scenario is shown in Fig. 8.3. You could first examine the network map on the management system to ensure that all network devices are up and running. Next, because there are several possible routes from *Kirk* to *Spock*, you would want to find which one was being used. Accordingly, the

TABLE 8.8

Object	Information Useful for Fault Management
ipRouteTable	IP routing table
ipNetToMediaTable	IP address translation table

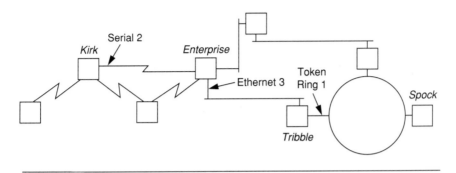

FIGURE 8.3
The network setup between *Kirk* and *Spock*.

fault management application could use ipRouteDest, ipRouteNextHop, and
ipRouteIfIndex to query *Kirk* and ask for the next hop to *Spock,* which happens
to be to the machine *Enterprise* through interface "Serial 2". The object
ipRouteDest is used to find the correct routing entry to reach *Spock,* ipRouteN-
extHop gives the address of the next hop, and ipRouteIfIndex gives the
outbound interface on the entity. The number returned by ipRouteIfIndex is
correlated to the ifIndex from the interfaces group. The string "Serial 2" could
then be found in ifDescr.

Your next step would be to ask *Enterprise* for the same information. You
learn that *Enterprise* routes to *Spock* by sending data through the device *Tribble*
via the interface "Ethernet 3". Next, you discover that *Tribble* sends data
directly to *Spock* via of interface "TokenRing 1". By performing this process,
you will have learned that *Kirk* does have a valid route to *Spock*.

Other IP group data that could help you solve this problem are the objects
listed in ipNetToMediaTable. These objects tell the mapping of IP addresses
to another protocol address. A common example is an ARP (Address Resolution Protocol) table that maps IP addresses to MAC (Media Access Control)
addresses. Returning to our example in the previous paragraph, let's say that
as part of solving the problem, the fault management application queried
Tribble for ipNetToMediaIfIndex, ipNetToMediaPhysAddress, and ipNet-
ToMediaNetAddress in each row of the ipNetToMediaTable. It happens that
one row of the table does contain an entry for *Spock,* found on interface
"TokenRing 1". You now know that *Tribble* has communicated with *Spock*.

A bit confused, you next might call the system administrator for *Spock* to
find out if any hardware or software on the system was recently changed. You
learn that the token ring interface on *Spock* was changed this morning. Hence,
the ipNetToMediaTable (or ARP cache, in this case) is out of date on *Tribble;*

the IP address to the token ring MAC address mapping is for the old interface board, which no longer exists. Therefore, you could decide to fix the trouble with Tribble by clearing the ARP cache. Then, the next time *Tribble* needs to contact *Spock, Tribble* will send an ARP and discover the correct translation between the IP address of *Spock* and the new token ring MAC address.

IP GROUP OBJECTS FOR CONFIGURATION MANAGEMENT

The IP group objects in Table 8.9 apply to configuration management.

Some network devices are set up to forward IP datagrams, such as routers. A configuration management application query to a device for the ipForwarding object can inform you about the functionality of the entity. For example, if the application queried a device for the system group object sysServices and found that a device services the network layer (layer 3), you might then want to learn if the device forwards IP datagrams with ipForwarding. In this case, an Appletalk router may return a value of sysServices that indicates it services the network layer, but ipForwarding may show you that the device does not route the IP.

As we saw in Chapter 3, knowing the network address, subnet mask, and broadcast address assigned to a device is invaluable for configuration management. The ipAddrTable gives information about the current IP addresses on the entity. Each row in the ipAddrTable is called an ipAddrEntry. Within each ipAddrEntry, the ipAdEntAddr and ipAdEntIfIndex tell the IP addresses and related interface, respectively. You can use ipAdEntIfIndex to correlate the ipAddrTable entry to an interfaces group ifTable entry. ipAdEntNetMask gives the subnet mask while ipAdEntBcastAddr tells the broadcast address. Note, however, that the MIB defines these objects as read-only, so for configuration management purposes an application or engineer can query for this information but cannot alter it.

The ipRouteTable does define many of its objects as read-write. For configuration management purposes, the application could enter new routes with ipRouteDest and change the route type with ipRouteType. Further,

TABLE 8.9

Object	Information Useful for Configuration Management
ipForwarding	If the device is set up to forward IP
ipAddrTable	IP addresses on the device
ipRouteTable	IP routing table

configuration of the routing metrics is possible by setting ipRouteMetric1, ipRouteMetric2, ipRouteMetric3, ipRouteMetric4, and ipRouteMetric5.

IP GROUP OBJECTS FOR PERFORMANCE MANAGEMENT

The IP group objects listed in Table 8.10 pertain to performance management.

Because of the large number of objects, we don't discuss each of them here. However, we do summarize some key objects in this section.

Using IP group objects, a performance management application can measure the percentage of IP traffic input and output by the entity. For example, the total packets received by the entity is available by computing the sum of ifInUcastPkts and ifInNUcastPkts for each interface and then dividing ipInReceives by this sum to find the percentage of IP datagrams received. A similar computation could be done using the object ipOutRequests for datagrams sent by the entity. Note that the object ipOutRequests only counts the number of datagrams sent by this entity, not the datagrams forwarded. By looking at the rate of change in the objects ipInReceives and ipOutRequests, you can find the rate at which this entity is receiving and sending IP datagrams.

TABLE 8.10

Object	Information Useful for Performance Management
ipInReceives	Rate of input datagrams
ipInHdrErrors	Rate of input header errors
ipInAddrErrors	Rate of input address errors
ipForwDatagrams	Rate of forwarded datagrams
ipInUnknownProtos	Rate of input datagrams for an unknown protocol
IpInDiscards	Rate of input datagrams discarded
ipInDelivers	Rate of input datagrams
ipOutRequests	Rate of output datagrams
ipOutDiscards	Rate of output datagrams discarded
ipOutNoRoutes	Rate of discards due to lack of routing information
ipRoutingDiscards	Rate of routing entries discarded
ipReasmReqds	Rate of datagrams received needing reassembly
ipReasmOKs	Rate datagrams successfully reassembled
ipReasmFails	Rate of fragmenttion reassembly failures
ipFragOKs	Rate of successful fragmentations
ipFragFails	Rate of unsuccessful fragmentations
ipFragCreates	Rate of fragments generated

The entity counts the number of times it has had to discard a datagram. The datagram may be discarded on input—the ipInDiscards object, or on output—the ipOutDiscards object. The discarding of a datagram may occur because of a lack of system resources or any other reason that did not permit the proper processing of the datagram.

Other error conditions can occur because a datagram comes into the entity with an invalid IP header—counted by the entity— the object ipInAddrErrors. A large percentage of IP packets that result in errors could lead to performance issues for an application using IP for delivery. The application can calculate the percentage of errors from IP datagrams as follows:

percent ip input errors =
$$\frac{(ipInDiscards + ipInHdrErrors + ipInAddrErrors)}{ipInReceives}$$

percent ip output errors =
$$\frac{(ipOutDiscards + ipOutHdrErrors + ipOutAddrErrors)}{ipOutRequests}$$

The interface group objects can also be used to compare the total number of packets output on all interfaces in relation to the rate of IP output errors. This can tell you if a large percentage of the packets output from the entity have resulted in IP output errors.

Some IP group objects can calculate errors that result from IP fragmentation. Computing percentages and rates of datagrams fragmented and their associated errors can prove insightful: It might be useful to know that a device is sending or receiving a large percentage of IP datagrams that are fragmented. Also, a large percentage of IP datagrams that result in fragmentation errors could have performance implications for an application using IP for network delivery.

The object ipRoutingDiscards can tell you if the entity is discarding valid IP routing entries because of a lack of resources. The rate at which IP routing entries are discarded can help you find out if the entity does not have enough resources to provide the necessary performance for the network. For example, if an entity is having to buffer a large number of datagrams, this can consume memory. If the entity runs out of buffers, it is possible that it may discard routing entries to make more buffers. But, the routing entries that were discarded may be necessary to forward the buffered datagrams. Then, the entity may have to rebuild routing entries it previously discarded, which takes more resources, or discard buffered datagrams because of a lack of routing information.

The object ipOutNoRoutes counts the number of times the entity did not have a valid route for a datagram. If the rate of this object increases, it may mean that the entity cannot forward a datagram to the destination. This object increases for datagrams sent and forwarded by the entity. For example, if the entity is forwarding datagrams to a destination and then a network fault occurs that results in the entity losing the route to the destination, this object will most likely increase until the source system realizes that the destination is no longer reachable through this entity.

If the entity is having to process a large number of datagrams for which it does not have a locally supported upper-layer protocol, measured by the object ipInUnknownProtos, this may also cause a performance concern. Typically, at this point the entity has received the datagram, checked it for errors, and determined that the destination was for a local IP address. If the entity now has to discard the datagram because it is destined for an unknown upper-layer protocol, this is a waste of resources. If this happens often or at a high rate, which can be tracked by checking the ipInUnknownProtos object over time, it may cause a performance problem.

Suppose, for example, that an organization has a collection of news servers that offer international news to their employees. An employee can connect a client to a news server and then can read new articles, search the archives for news items, save news articles locally, and so forth. The IP carries the packets between the news servers and the clients. The upper-layer protocol that guarantees that the IP datagrams arrive reliably was written by the organization, and is only available on the news servers. If an employee tries to connect a client to a system that does not support the upper-layer protocol used by the news servers, then the object ipInUnknownProtos will increase. If many clients repeatedly try to connect to a server that does not support the upper-layer protocol, this may cause a performance problem.

ipForwDatagrams tells the forwarding rate of the device with respect to IP datagrams. If the system is polled twice, once at time x (in seconds) and then again at time y (in seconds), the following formula shows the IP packet forwarding rate per second:

$$\text{ip-forwarding-rate} = \frac{(\text{ipForwDatagrams}_y - \text{ipForwDatagrams}_x)}{y - x}$$

The rate of IP packets received by the system is found as follows:

$$\text{ip-input-rate} = \frac{(\text{ipInReceives}_y - \text{ipInReceives}_x)}{y - x}$$

By having the application monitor these rates, you can determine if the system is forwarding IP packets fast enough to satisfy network requirements. ipInReceives gives the total number of IP packets received by the entity. If the entity then is forwarding these packets, the IP forwarding rate should be equal to the IP input rate. To make this calculation more accurate, subtract the rate of IP input errors and IP packets delivered to this system. Doing this means you

TABLE 8.11

Object	Information Useful for Accounting Management
ipOutRequests	Number of IP packet sent
ipInDelivers	Number of IP packets received

compare the forwarding rate only to the rate of IP packets received that were either not errors or for this entity itself.

IP GROUP OBJECTS FOR ACCOUNTING MANAGEMENT

The IP group objects in Table 8.11 pertain to accounting management.

ipOutRequests and ipInDelivers tell the total number of IP packets an entity has sent and received, respectively, information that can be important for billing network users. For accounting purposes, use ipInDelivers; it gives the number of IP packets delivered to upper-layer protocols and applications without error.

8.6 The ICMP Group

ICMP[2] is a protocol that carries error and control messages for IP devices. The *ICMP group* contains objects that give information about the ICMP on the entity. All of its objects, listed in Table 8.12 apply to performance management.

Because of the large number of objects that apply to this application, we don't discuss them individually here. We do, however, summarize several of the objects in this section.

The entity must process every ICMP packet received; doing this can negatively affect overall entity performance. While during periods of normal network traffic the processing power consumed may be minimal, at busier times sending large numbers of ICMP packets could require enough resources to notice-ably hamper an entity's performance. Further, some ICMP packets received, for

[2]ICMP is defined in *RFC* 792.

TABLE 8.12

Object	Information Useful for Performance Management
icmpInMsgs	Rate of input messages
icmpInErrors	Rate of input errors
icmpInDestUnreachs	Rate of input Destination Unreachable messages
icmpInTimeExcds	Rate of input Time Exceeded messages
icmpInParmProbs	Rate of input Parameter Problem messages
icmpInSrcQuenchs	Rate of input Source Quench messages
icmpInRedirects	Rate of input Redirect messages
icmpInEchos	Rate of input Echo messages
icmpInEchoReps	Rate of input Echo Reply messages
icmpInTimestamps	Rate of input Timestamp messages
icmpInTimestampReps	Rate of input Timestamp Reply messages
icmInAddrMasks	Rate of input Address Mask Request messages
icmpInAddrMaskReps	Rate of input Address Mask Reply messages
icmpOutMsgs	Rate of output messages
icmpOutErrors	Rate of output errors
icmpOutDestUnreachs	Rate of output Destination Unreachable messages
icmpOutTimeExcds	Rate of output Time Exceeded messages
icmpOutParmProbs	Rate of output Parameter Problem messages
icmpOutSrcQuenchs	Rate of output Source Quench messages
icmpOutRedirects	Rate of output Redirect messages
icmpOutEchos	Rate of output Echo messages
icmpOutEchoReps	Rate of output Echo Reply messages
icmpOutTimestamps	Rate of output Timestamp messages
icmpOutTimestampReps	Rate of output Timestamp Reply messages
icmpOutAddrMasks	Rate of output Address Mask Request messages
icmpOutAddrMaskReps	Rate of output Address Mask Reply messages

instance an Echo, require a response to be built, which consumes more processing power. Similarly, the generation of new ICMP packets, such as a Source Quench, by the entity can result in overloading available resources.

For the application to calculate the percentage of ICMP packets received and sent, it first must know the total number of packets received and sent by the entity. As we saw in Section 8.3, this is done by finding the total of packets input and packets output from each interface. We then would divide this sum by icmpInMsgs and icmpOutMsgs to arrive at the percentage of total ICMP packets received or sent. By having the application poll multiple times for these objects, you can discover the rate at which ICMP packets go in and out of the entity. Note the fact that an entity is receiving or sending many ICMP packets does not necessarily mean a performance problem exists, but your having these statistics might help you solve a future related problem.

Consider a setup in which a user complains about the slow performance of a remote login session to a host called *Einstein.* In response, you could check the fault management tool to see if a fault exists between the user and *Einstein.* Not finding a fault, you then could use the performance management application to graph the processor load on *Einstein.* Doing this, you discover that the processor load is very high, almost 70 percent, with spikes reaching above 90 percent. You then could check the number of users and processes on *Einstein,* whereupon you discover only a small number of each.

Still trying to isolate the problem, you next could produce a graph showing the packet rate entering and leaving *Einstein.* It turns out that the packet rate is high, reaching almost to the maximum performance of the interface board. Looking more closely, you find that many of the packets are ICMP. Again you check the system processes, this time finding one that seems to be continuously sending ICMP Echo packets (pings) to every system on the network. The purpose of this action is to verify the reachability of every system on the data network from *Einstein;* however, by doing so, the process is consuming enough system resources to cause a performance problem on *Einstein.*

ICMP group objects also can show the number of each different ICMP packet type. Knowing the rate of icmpInEchos, icmpOutEchos, icmpInEchoReps, and icmpOutEchoReps, you could isolate performance problems such as that with *Einstein.* An entity receiving a large number of icmpInSrcQuenchs could indicate oncoming congestion on the network. Likewise, an entity sending a large number of icmpOutSrcQuenchs may mean the entity is running out of resources. Further, if an entity is sending or receiving many IP errors, then the application could use icmpInErrors and icmpOutErrors to determine if ICMP packets are causing the problem.

8.7 The TCP Group

The TCP is a transport protocol that provides reliable connections between applications. Many implementations of the TCP include enhancements to deal with flow control, network congestion, and the retransmission of lost segments.

TCP group objects can help in configuration, performance, and accounting management. As with the IP group, this group is subdivided, as follows:

1. General objects about the TCP on the system
2. A table of values for each current TCP connection. This table changes with the start or end of a TCP connection.

The structure of the TCP group is shown in Fig. 8.4.

TCP GROUP OBJECTS FOR CONFIGURATION MANAGEMENT

The TCP group objects in Table 8.13 apply to configuration management.

The configuration of the TCP retransmission algorithm and its associated timers can drastically affect the performance of the applications that use this protocol for transport. If different systems use different retransmission schemes, network congestion or unfair distribution of bandwidth could result. For example, a system that uses a constant retransmission timer may tend to consume unnecessary bandwidth in comparison to one that uses Van Jacobson's algorithm[3]. By having the application query for tcpRtoAlgorithm,

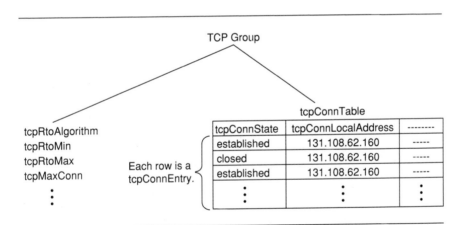

FIGURE 8.4
The structure of the TCP group. Note that not all the objects in each section are shown.

[3]For further information on the TCP and retransmission issues, refer to the paper by Van Jacobson titled *Congestion Avoidance and Control*.

TABLE 8.13

Object	Information Useful for Configuration Management
tcpRtoAlgorithm	TCP retransmission algorithm
tcpRtoMin	Smallest TCP retransmission timeout
tcpRtoMax	Largest TCP retransmission timeout
tcpMaxConn	Total TCP connections allowed
tcpCurrEstab	Number of current TCP connections

tcpRtoMin, and tcpRtoMax, you could learn if the current configuration of the TCP works well in your system's network environment.

These objects provide useful information, but modifying them may require some work or even be impossible. On some systems, modification of the TCP retransmission timers requires rebuilding the operating system. Often, however, the TCP retransmission algorithm is an integral part of the operating system of a device and cannot be altered.

tcpMaxConn can help you configure a network to handle the necessary number of remote TCP connections. If the total of all possible TCP connections do not satisfy user demand, another system might be needed. Or, if the system allows expansion, you might find that you have to add the resources to permit more TCP connections. Note that the current number of connections, found in tcpCurrEstab, can influence your decision on the total number of needed TCP connections.

The existing number of TCP connections to a system can also affect the system's performance. If a system that can handle 10 remote login sessions tries to serve one hundred such sessions, performance most likely will be hurt.

TCP GROUP OBJECTS FOR PERFORMANCE MANAGEMENT

The TCP group objects in Table 8.14 pertain to performance management.

An attempt to establish a TCP connection can fail for a variety of reasons; for example, the destination system may not exist or the network may have a fault. Your knowing the number of rejected attempts at making a connection can help you quantify network reliability, where fewer rejections might indicate a more reliable network. Likewise, a situation in which TCP ends many established sessions in a reset condition might also reflect an unreliable network. tcpAttemptFails and tcpEstabResets can help measure this network rejection rate.

tcpRetransSegs gives the number of TCP segments the system has re-sent. The retransmission of a TCP segment does not directly reflect a performance

TABLE 8.14

Object	Information Useful for Performance Management
tcpAttempt Fails	Number of failed attempts to make a connection
tcpEstabResets	Number of resets from established connection
tcpRetransSegs	Number of segments retransmitted
tcpInErrs	Number of packets received in error
tcpOutRsts	Number of times TCP tried to reset a connection
tcpInSegs	Rate of input TCP segments
tcpOutSegs	Rate of output TCP segments

problem; however, the number of retransmissions can tell you if the entity is having to send multiple copies of data in an effort to ensure reliability.

If the system is receiving TCP segments in error, the value of tcpInErrs will increase. Trouble receiving segments and an increase in this object might be caused by the source system encapsulating the segments wrong, a network device forwarding the segment in error, or any number of other reasons. In most situations, this value of this object will not rise independently, but rather as a result of some other error on the system.

tcpOutRsts gives the number of times the entity has tried to reset a connection. A condition in which the entity is attempting to reset a connection could result from network unreliability, a user request to do so, or a resource problem; the exact reasons for sending a reset can be unique to an entity. By understanding the TCP on the entity, you will be better able to understand the use of this object.

Having the application poll tcpInSegs and tcpOutSegs over time can enable you to check the rate of TCP segments as they enter and leave the entity. This rate may affect the performance of the entity or an application relying on TCP for transport.

TCP GROUP OBJECTS FOR ACCOUNTING MANAGEMENT

The TCP group objects in Table 8.15 apply to accounting management.

An organization may want to know the number of TCP connections to and from a system in order to evaluate current usage of network resources. Such an evaluation could lead to the purchase of additional systems or a system

TABLE 8.15

Object	Information Useful for Accounting Management
tcpActiveOpens	Number of times this system has opened a connection
tcpPassiveOpens	Number of times this system has received a request to open a connection
tcpInSegs	Total number of TCP segments received
tcpOutSegs	Total number of TCP segments sent
tcpConnTable	Current TCP connections

reconfiguration. tcpActiveOpens and tcpPassiveOpens give the total number of times a connection was made from or to the system, respectively.

tcpInSegs and tcpOutSegs together count TCP segments in and out of the entity, respectively, information that can be significant in network billing.

tcpConnTable gives the state of current TCP connections, the local TCP port and address, and the remote TCP port and address. These values pertain to the current state of the TCP on the entity and may change at any instant. Nevertheless, by having the accounting management application poll for the object tcpConRemAddress, you can determine the current remote system addresses of a TCP connection. (Note that the information obtained is only the remote system address, not the remote user.) If the application were to poll an entity for this object every 15 minutes, system administrators could determine which remote systems use their resources and for what duration. (Of course, the granularity of the duration shown is only as fine as the polling interval.) The application then could generate bills for using the local entity for those users that own the remote systems and use the local entity.

tcpConnTable also contains information about the source and destination TCP port for each current connection. Many popular TCP applications use well-defined ports, making it possible to track which application is making or receiving the TCP connection. The port number differentiates between a remote login application such as *telnet* and a file transfer application like *ftp*. This data can be useful for accounting purposes to determine the reason for TCP connections to and from an entity.

TCP GROUP OBJECTS FOR SECURITY MANAGEMENT

Information in the tcpConnTable, discussed in the previous paragraph, also can be used in security management to track which remote systems access resources via TCP. This data can form the basis of reports to show that the entity has not allowed any connections from foreign or unrestricted systems. The polling interval would greatly influence the effectiveness of such a report—an intruder may need only a few seconds to gather its information before breaking the connection. If a poll of the table did not occur within those few seconds, all record of the intrusion would be lost.

8.8 The UDP Group

The UDP is a transport layer protocol like the TCP but with a less rigorous functional requirement than the TCP has. Unlike the TCP, the UDP does not guarantee reliability or set up connections; instead, it uses a stream of datagrams to transport information. Further, most UDP implementations do not have the enhancements of the TCP. Because of this, the *UDP group* contains a limited number of objects.

Objects in the UDP group are subdivided as follows:

1. Information about the UDP on this entity
2. Entries about the current UDP applications accepting datagrams on the entity

The structure of the UDP group is shown in Fig. 8.5.

Because the UDP does not establish connections, the UDP table does not give data about the current connections—they would never exist. Instead, the table tells about each listening local port and related network address.

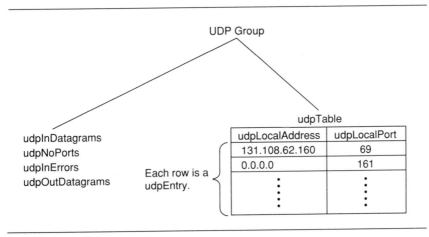

FIGURE 8.5
The structure of the UDP group.

UDP group objects can help in performance and accounting management. This functionality is similar to that of the TCP group objects for the same areas of network management.

UDP GROUP OBJECTS FOR PERFORMANCE MANAGEMENT

The UDP group objects in Table 8.16 apply to performance management.

Processing UDP datagrams can affect the performance of the entity, so polling for udpInDatagrams and udpOutDatagrams over time can yield valuable data in the form of the input and output rate of datagrams.

udpNoPorts tells you when an entity is receiving datagrams for an unknown application. If the rate of these datagrams is significant, a performance problem on the entity could result. An entity can commonly receive datagrams in this manner when an UDP application uses IP broadcast packets to deliver information. Upon seeing an IP broadcast, every IP device picks up the broadcast packet and delivers it to the UDP. Only those systems with the application running and the proper UDP port listening receive the packet; all others report this packet in the udpNoPorts object.

For example, the trivial file transfer protocol (TFTP)[4] uses UDP to allow a device to send or receive a single file without using a password. A TFTP server offers a file by listening on a UDP port for a TFTP client asking for the file. In many cases, a TFTP client will send an IP broadcast to find a TFTP server on the network. Systems that have such a server listening will receive the broadcast and send the file to the client, if possible. All other IP hosts that are not listening on the TFTP port will increment their udpNoPorts object.

As in IP and TCP, udpInErrors can tell you about specific errors on the network. A UDP datagram may contain an error for many reasons, including

TABLE 8.16

Object	Information Useful for Performance Management
udpInDatagrams	Rate of input datagrams
udpOutDatagrams	Rate of output datagrams
udpNoPorts	Rate of datagrams that were not sent to to a valid port
udpInErrors	Rate of UDP datagrams received in error

[4]TFTP is defined in RFC 783.

software or link errors or a faulty network device. A system receiving many datagrams that count as udpInErrors could contribute to the poor performance of an application in receiving information. For example, SNMP uses UDP for transport. If the network management system is having trouble receiving SNMP datagrams from a remote system, the local udpInErrors counter could indicate that the datagram containing the SNMP information possibly did not make it across the network successfully.

UDP GROUP OBJECTS FOR ACCOUNTING MANAGEMENT

The UDP group objects in Table 8.17 pertain to accounting management.

You can use udpInDatagrams and udpOutDatagrams to determine how many UDP datagrams an entity has sent and received. In this way, you can learn the demand for the UDP and the applications that use it on the entity.

udpTable contains objects similar to those found in tcpConnTable. This table is a collection of udpEntry entries, each of which contains two objects: udpLocalAddress and udpLocalPort. udpLocalAddress gives the local IP address for the listening port; udpLocalPort gives the port number. However, because the UDP is not a connection-based protocol, the entries in the udpTable remain valid for the time that the application listens on a port. This facility provides you with the means to monitor which services the network offers on an entity basis. You could check where these services exist on the network to find out if the appropriate network resources exist.

UDP GROUP OBJECTS FOR CONFIGURATION MANAGEMENT

Monitoring of available network services falls into the realm of configuration management. By checking with the udpTable, you can determine if the entity's applications are set up correctly. For example, if an entity is known to have an application that offers remote printing on a known UDP port, you could easily verify this configuration information using the udpTable.

TABLE 8.17

Object	Information Useful for Accounting Management
udpInDatagrams	Total number of UDP datagrams received
udpOutDatagrams	Total number of UDP datagrams sent
udpTable	Current UDP ports accepting datagrams

UDP GROUP OBJECTS FOR SECURITY MANAGEMENT

Security management also can use the information in the udpTable. In the same way that a security management application can poll for tcpConnTable information to check for unauthorized access, the application can check to ensure an entity does not run an unsecured application using the UDP. Suppose for example an organization has decided that the application *Find-Employee-Salary* is to be run only on one specific machine. *Find-Employee-Salary* listens for requests to find an employees salary on a specific UDP port. The security management tool could check the udpTable on all systems to check if this local port is listening, thus helping to control access to sensitive information.

8.9 The EGP Group

The EGP[5] group is a protocol that tells an IP network device about the reachability of other IP networks. It doesn't give the entire route to another network, but it does enable a device to know in which direction a network exists. IP networks can be grouped into logical areas called *autonomous systems*. An autonomous system is usually one network and its associated subnets or a collection of networks and sub-networks under the same administration. Two network devices in two different autonomous systems can share reachability information via EGP.

The network devices that communicate with the EGP between autonomous systems are called *EGP neighbors*. Each EGP process has a one-to-one relationship with each neighbor. Each EGP neighbor speaks a hello protocol that periodically informs other neighbors that it is still active. When the system queries for the neighbor's reachability information, it is performing an *EGP poll*.

For example, consider two networks, A and B, each with an EGP neighbor communicating to the other network (see Fig. 8.6). EGP data may allow a device within network A to know the best way to get to network B and visa-versa. However, that device will not know how to reach a specific destination or sub-network in network B; it will know only the direction of all of network B.

EGP group objects are subdivided, as follows (see Fig. 8.7):

1. Information about the EGP on this entity. These objects pertain to configuration, performance, and accounting management.
2. A table of entries that contains information about a unique EGP neighbor. Information in this table is useful in fault, configuration, performance, and accounting management.

---

[5]EGP is defined in RFC 904.

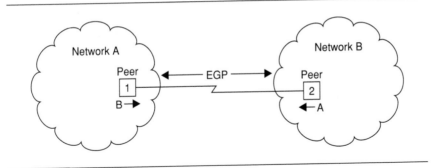

FIGURE 8.6
EGP peer 1 knows about the reachability of network B, while EGP peer 2
knows about the reachability of network A.

EGP GROUP OBJECTS FOR FAULT MANAGEMENT

The EGP group objects in Table 8.18 pertain to fault management.

Each of these objects reside in the EGP neighbor table. The state of an
EGP neighbor can provide information about how routing information is
injected into an autonomous system. The fault management application could
use egpNeighState to find the current state of an EGP neighbor. If a neighbor

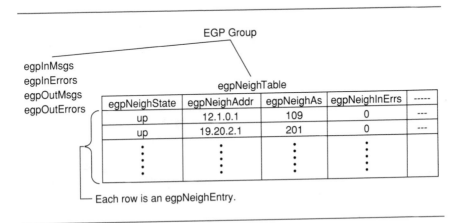

FIGURE 8.7
The structure of the EGP group. Note that not every column of the egpNeighTable
is shown.

TABLE 8.18

Object	Information Useful for Fault Management
egpNeighState	State of each EGP neighbor
egpNeighStateUps	When an EGP neighbor enters an UP state
egpNeighStateDowns	When an EGP neighbor enters a DOWN state

is up, then it should be sending information about the reachability of networks to the local EGP process. Knowing when a neighbor enters the up state can tell you about new routing information that may enter the autonomous system. Similarly, knowing when a neighbor stops communicating and enters the down state could be helpful in solving a routing problem. As we saw in Chapter 7 with SNMP, when a neighbor enters the down state, the entity sends a trap message.

EGP GROUP OBJECTS FOR CONFIGURATION MANAGEMENT

The EGP group objects in Table 8.19 apply to configuration management.

egpAs gives the autonomous system number for the local EGP entity. All the other listed objects tell about the configuration of a specific EGP neighbor. This information, polled by the configuration management application, can keep you informed about the setup of the EGP and the routing information entering or leaving the current autonomous system.

The application can use egpNeighEventTrigger to start or stop communication with an EGP neighbor. This object enables you to control the EGP

TABLE 8.19

Object	Information Useful for Configuration Management
egpNeighState	State of each EGP neighbor
egpNeighAddr	The EGP neighbor IP address
egpNeighAs	The EGP neighbor autonomous system
egpNeighIntervalHello	The EGP hello interval
egpNeighIntervalPoll	The EGP poll interval
egpNeighMode	The EGP polling mode
egpNeighEventTrigger	Permits the starting or stopping of communication
egpAs	The local EGP autonomous system

process on the system. Note that setting the object does not start the EGP on the entity, but rather restarts communication with an existing neighbor. This is the only object in the EGP group that can be set by the network engineer via a SNMP Set-Request. In a common example, consider a network device that has two EGP neighbors, each providing reachability information to many IP networks. The primary EGP session is up and passing reachability information into the local autonomous system; the secondary EGP session is idle. Although the primary path out of the local autonomous system is preferred because of cost and security considerations, at some point the primary EGP communication fails. Upon discovering this failure, you would probably attempt to restart communication. If this effort failed, you then could use the egpNeighTrigger-Event object to start the secondary EGP session.

EGP GROUP OBJECTS FOR PERFORMANCE MANAGEMENT

Failure of the EGP communication in the example given in the previous section might have resulted from a failure on a circuit. In this case, the error rate for EGP information received might have increased before the failure. A performance management application, monitoring this error rate, could have informed you if the rate increased. The EGP group objects in Table 8.20 apply to performance management.

TABLE 8.20

Object	Information Useful for Performance Management
egpInMsgs	Rate of messages received
egpInErrors	Rate of errors received
egpOutMsgs	Rate of messages sent
egpOutErrors	Rate of messages not sent because of error
egpNeighInMsgs	Rate of messages received from this EGP neighbor
egpNeighInErrs	Rate of errors received from this EGP neighbor
egpNeighOutMsgs	Rate of messages sent to this EGP neighbor
egpNeighOutErrs	Rate of messages not sent to this EGP neighbor because of error
egpNeighInErrMsgs	Rate of EGP error messages received from this EGP neighbor
egpNeighOutErrMsgs	Rate of EGP error messages sent to this EGP neighbor

As we saw in Section 8.3, to find a rate using an object requires multiple polls of the object. The performance management application could poll multiple times for an object and then divide the difference in the values of the object by the time elapsed between polls. This obtains the rate of change for an object.

egpInMsgs and egpOutMsgs enable you to watch the rate of EGP messages entering and leaving the entity. Usually, this rate will be insignificant, but during periods of network instability between EGP neighbors, it could climb. When this happens, processing EGP messages may consume too many resources and so cause slow performance on the entity. Further, the EGP messages themselves may take up bandwidth on a serial link, thus causing poor or delayed transmission of data traversing the same link.

An increase in egpInErrors and egpOutErrors may coincide with the increase in the number of messages sent and received by the entity. If a message is received in error and a valid response isn't sent, the source EGP neighbor may retransmit the message. When the entity can't send valid EGP messages due to resource limitations, egpOutErrors will increase. Consequently, when the rate of egpInMsgs nears the rate of egpOutErrors, the entity probably is suffering difficulty in building and sending EGP messages. A lack of entity resources such as memory or processing power could cause this phenomenon.

A situation in which an EGP is causing performance issues on the entity or on an attached serial link requires you to isolate which neighbor is creating the problem. Using egpNeighInMsgs, egpNeighInErrs, egpNeighOutMsgs, and egpNeighOutErrs, you can compute the rate of input and output messages and the errors for each neighbor.

By examining the rate of increase in egpNeighInErrMsgs and egpNeighOutErrMsgs, you can determine when EGP neighbors are receiving and sending valid EGP error messages. An increase in the rate of these error messages may indicate a misconfiguration or a change in the future performance of the EGP on this neighbor.

8.10 The CMOT Group

The *CMOT group* exists only for historical reasons. Previously, it was seen as a protocol to help in the transition from SNMP to CMIS/CMIP. As we described in Chapter 7, CMOT is no longer considered in this light, so there are no objects in this group.

8.11 The Transmission Group

The *transmission group* gives you information about the specific media that underlie the interfaces on a system. When the Internet standards for managing the various types of media are defined, this group will be a prefix for this information. However, at the time of this writing, no objects exist in this group.

8.12 The SNMP Group

The *SNMP group* gives information about, among other things, the SNMP errors and packets entering and leaving the entity. This last group in the MIB is helpful in all five areas of network management. Fault management applications watching for SNMP problems can find useful the number of SNMP errors and their frequency, while performance management applications can calculate the rate of SNMP packets entering and leaving the entity. Accounting management applications can use these objects to find the exact number of SNMP packets sent to or received by the entity. And finally, some of the other SNMP objects can be helpful in accomplishing security and configuration management.

SNMP GROUP OBJECTS FOR FAULT MANAGEMENT

The SNMP group objects in Table 8.21 apply to fault management.

Each object gives information about errors concerning the SNMP. RFC 1157 defines each of these errors. While an agent's receiving or sending these errors might not indicate a problem with the network itself, they may tell you that an entity is not handling SNMP packets properly. The number and types of errors also can indicate that the entity is receiving SNMP packets with errors from network devices. The solutions to these errors often reside in the configuration either of the SNMP manager or of the agent. If reconfiguration does not alleviate these errors, the problem might lie within the implementation of the SNMP on the manager or agent.

TABLE 8.21

Object	Information Useful for Fault Management
snmpInASNParseErrs	Total input ASN errors
snmpInTooBigs	Total input 'tooBig' errors
snmpInNoSuchNames	Total input 'noSuchName' errors
snmpInBadValues	Total input 'badValue' errors
snmpInReadOnlys	Total input 'readOnly' errors
snmpInGenErrs	Total input 'genErr' errors
snmpOutTooBigs	Total output 'tooBig' errors
snmpOutNoSuchNames	Total output 'noSuchName' errors
snmpOutBadValues	Total output 'badValue' errors
snmpOutGenErrs	Total output 'genErr' errors

SNMP GROUP OBJECTS FOR PERFORMANCE MANAGEMENT

The SNMP objects in Table 8.22 apply to performance management.

Like any other entity activity, the SNMP can affect system performance. If you want to know what percentage of resources an entity is using to handle the SNMP, you can find the rate of SNMP packets input and output using snmpInPkts and snmpOutPkts. The remainder of objects listed in the table enable you to find the type of SNMP packets the entity is handling. Monitoring the rates of these objects can suggest the cause of a high SNMP packet input or output rate. For example, a high rate of snmpInGetRequests and snmpOut-GetResponses may indicate that a manager is currently gathering information from the entity.

SNMP GROUP OBJECTS FOR ACCOUNTING MANAGEMENT

Some of the same objects useful for performance management also apply to accounting management, as shown in Table 8.23.

Instead of using these objects to find the rate at which packets enter and leave the entity, as in performance management, accounting management applications can use them to find a total number for each type of SNMP packet sent and received, information that can be useful for network billing.

If the network billing model calculates costs based upon packets sent or received by a billing group, this data can help compute the total number of SNMP packets into and out of the billing group. For example, suppose the

TABLE 8.22

Object	Information Useful for Performance Management
snmpInPkts	Rate of SNMP packets input
snmpOutPkts	Rate of SNMP packets sent
snmpInTotalReqVars	Rate of Get/Get-Next Requests input
snmpInTotalSetVars	Rate of Set-Requests input
snmpInGetRequests	Rate of Get-Requests input
snmpInGetNexts	Rate of Get-Next-Requests input
snmpInSetRequests	Rate of Set-Requests input
snmpInGetResponses	Rate of Get-Responses input
snmpInTraps	Rate of Traps input
snmpOutGetRequests	Rate of Get-Requests output
snmpOutGetNexts	Rate of Get-Next-Requests output
snmpOutSetRequests	Rate of Set-Requests output
snmpOutGetResponses	Rate of Get-Responses output
snmpOutTraps	Rate of Traps output

TABLE 8.23

Object	Information Useful for Accounting Management
snmpInPkts	Total SNMP packets input
snmpOutPkts	Total SNMP packets sent
snmpInTraps	Total Traps input
snmpOutTraps	Total Traps output

marketing department of a company receives a bill each month for the number of packets it receives from the network. The marketing department network is divided from the main network by two network devices, both of which are managed by an outside organization responsible for the network. The community strings configured in the two network devices are known only by the outside managing organization, ensuring no other users can query the devices via SNMP. Therefore, because the billing process computes costs based on packets received, the SNMP packets these two devices receive should not be included in the final bill for the marketing department. snmpInPkts and snmpInTraps can give the number of packets that should be subtracted from that final bill.

SNMP GROUP OBJECTS FOR SECURITY MANAGEMENT

The SNMP group objects in Table 8.24 apply to security management.

As we learned in Chapter 4, security management involves tracking failed authentication attempts. The actions taken to do this might include checking for unsuccessful password entries for a computer login or for invalid community

TABLE 8.24

Object	Information Useful for Security Management
snmpInBadCommunityNames	Total number of packets with a wrong community string
snmpInBadCommunityUses	Total number of packets with community strings that did not allow the requested operation

strings in the SNMP. snmpInBadCommunityNames counts the number of times a user or application, when attempting to communicate with the SNMP on an entity, does not give the correct community string. As discussed in Chapter 7, when an entity receives an invalid community string, it also might send a SNMP Authentication Failure Trap message to a manager. We discuss whether to configure for this action in the next subsection.

snmpInBadCommunityUses counts the number of times an SNMP packet was received that had a community string that did not allow the requested operation. In many network devices, different community strings can be set up for different operations. For example, one community string might authorize the Get-Request and Get-Next-Request operations; another might allow Get-Request, Get-Next-Request, and Set-Request operations. An organization that manages a network device might know the community string that allows all SNMP operations—Get-Request, Get-Next-Request, and Set-Request—but could elect to allow for public use only the community string that allows access to Get-Request and Get-Next-Request operations. In this case, it would do this to ensure that only employees in the organization could configure the network devices via Set-Request operations.

If the values of either of these two objects were to increase, the security management application could warn you via a message or pop-up window. This event also could be logged in the relational database for future analysis. Such an analysis could show that the events occur on a timely basis, which could lead you to conclude that perhaps a management station polling the device doesn't know the proper community string.

SNMP GROUP OBJECTS FOR CONFIGURATION MANAGEMENT

The following SNMP group object applies to configuration management: snmpEnableAuthenTraps.

By definition, an entity must have the ability to send an SNMP Authentication Failure trap when it receives a SNMP packet with an incorrect community string. However, because community strings are in ASCII, this procedure can pose potentially dangerous security problems. Because of these security concerns, you can override the entity and set snmpEnableAuthenTraps to enable—send—or disable—don't send—the trap.

Summary

The standard MIB for SNMP—RFC 1213—contains a wealth of information useful in managing a data network, all of which is currently available from many network devices. Because of the copious amounts of data in the MIB, deciphering which objects help in which areas of network management often can be overwhelming and difficult. To help you with this, we used this chapter to take a close look at RFC 1213, examining each group within the MIB and offering guidance regarding the specific objects useful for each functional area of network management.

For Further Study

Case, J., M. Fedor, M. Schoffstall, and C. Davin, RFC 1157, *Simple Network Management Protocol (SNMP)*, May 1990.

Jacobson, V., *Congestion Avoidance and Control,* Proceedings of the ACM, SIG-COMM '88, Volume 18, Number 4, August 1988.

McCloghrie, K., and M. Rose, RFC 1156, *Management Information Base for Network Management for TCP/IP-based internets,* May 1990.

McCloghrie, K., and M. Rose, RFC 1213, *Management Information Base for Network Management for TCP/IP-based internets: MIB-II,* March 1991.

Mills, D., RFC 904, *Exterior Gateway Protocol specification,* April 1984.

Postel, J., RFC 792, *Internet Control Message Protocol,* September 1981.

Rose, M., and K. McCloghrie, RFC 1155, *Structure and Identification of Management Information for TCP/IP-based Internets,* May 1990.

Rose, M., and K. McCloghrie, RFC 1212, *Concise MIB Definitions,* March 1991.

Sollins, K., RFC 783, *TFTP Protocol (revision 2),* June 1981.

9

Productivity Tools

In this chapter:
- Tools for using a MIB
- Tools for presenting information
- Tools for helping troubleshoot network problems

A network management system comprises a set of software tools to help the network engineer manage a data network. However, the system also can include many other features helpful to the engineer that do not directly relate to a specific functional area of network management. While this additional functionality is not a strict requirement for a system to operate acceptably, the addition of certain tools can significantly enhance the productivity of the engineer and hence, the efficiency of the system.

For example, the engineer might need a way to manipulate and examine the objects in a MIB. After using MIB objects to gather information from a device, the engineer could use presentation tools to produce logs, graphs, and reports of the data. The engineer further could use problem-solving tools to analyze the data gathered from network devices and offer possible solutions.

In this chapter, we look at three types of productivity tools beneficial on a network management system:

1. MIB tools—a compiler, a browser tool, an alias tool, and a query tool

2. Presentation tools—a centralized log, a report writer, and a graphics package

3. Problem-solving tools—a trouble-tracking system and an expert system

Although it would be desirable for a system to possess a complete set of such tools, none are dependent on the others; they can exist independently. Further, while we discuss many common tools, we want to stress that others might exist or could be developed for specific network environments. At the time of this writing, there are already tools on the market that incorporate many features we describe in this chapter. We recommend that when you are purchasing or developing a network management system, you consider including these some or all of these productivity tools, depending on how you want the system to help you perform network management.

9.1 MIB Tools

Tools to manipulate MIB information can be helpful on a network management system. These tools might include the following:

- A MIB compiler, which loads MIBs into the system, that can assist you in obtaining necessary data from the inevitably large variety of devices on the network. This facility also can provide you with a means to relate MIB attributes to graphical elements on the network map.
- A MIB browser, an electronic means of browsing the MIB after it has been loaded in order to find specific information
- A MIB alias tool for associating potentially confusing MIB object names to references that are more familiar to you
- A MIB query tool to poll agents in the network devices in order to examine the values returned, which can help you decide if polling for an object is useful.

We examine each of these tools in more depth next.

MIB COMPILER

A *MIB compiler* takes in a file in RFC 1155 format and converts it for use with the network management system. Customized versions of a MIB are usually preferred because they perform operations such as searches and lookups faster than an ASCII file can. You might need to use the MIB compiler to incorporate a new vendor-specific MIB or an update of an existing MIB file. This function should be simple to use. Perhaps the system has an input field that allows a user to specify the name of the ASCII MIB file. In this case, the compiler could automatically read in this file and allow you to view the specific objects; an example of this tool is shown in Fig. 9.1. These objects can apply to any of the five functional areas of network management.

For example, suppose you wanted to learn the current number of active stations or a wiring hub, information that is important for accounting and performance issues. Using the standard MIB, this information is not available. However, you could add the vendor-specific MIB for the wiring hub to the network management system and thus be able to retrieve this data.

In another case, the wiring hub could allow for the activation and deactivation of a port by performing a SNMP Set-Request on a vendor-specific MIB object. As we saw in Chapter 2, a fault management tool could use this object

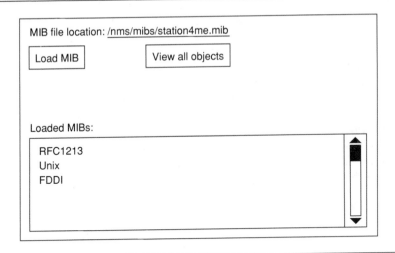

FIGURE 9.1
A tool that compiles MIBs into the network management system.

to shut off a faulty port while a configuration management tool could use it to set up the hub.

Although accessing vendor-specific MIB information is important, you often might find it useful to relate the objects to the network map. Suppose that in the same wiring hub MIB, there is an object that shows the input error rate on each port. You could set up a process to gather this input error rate data and store it in the relational database for performance management (we described this process in Chapter 5). However, you could find it helpful to have the port and its associated representation on the network map display a graphic signal if a high input error rate occurs. The performance management application probably could not perform this function because, as written, it doesn't understand the vendor-specific MIB object. Building a relationship between a specific MIB object and a graphical element is a sophisticated way to use MIB information.

Let's look at still another example. Suppose you want to set up the network management system to monitor the input error rate on a fiber-distributed data interface (FDDI) on a file server. You decide that if the input error rate exceeds two percent, you would want the device on the network map to flash the icon depicting the file server. As you can see, setting up such arbitrary relationships between MIB objects and the network map can help your productivity: Having the network management system inform you when the input error rate on the FDDI ring exceeds two percent would free you to work on other tasks until you are alerted.

Still, this functionality might not provide all the necessary features you want. For example, you might want to associate multiple MIB objects and their decrease, increase, or change of state to a graphical element. Consider a situation in which you manage a network of T-1 multiplexers interconnecting LANs in many cities. Using objects in the standard MIB, such as those in the interface table, the fault management application could cause links with errors to flash on the network map. For T-1 links, an important datum from the multiplexers is a standard metric called Severely Errored Seconds. Now, this information is not available through the standard MIB, but is available through the T-1 MIB.[1] Further, you decide you want a link on the network map to flash when the Severely Errored Seconds object reaches a defined threshold. To provide this functionality, the network management system first must learn about the T-1 MIB. Then, you would need a means of telling the system that when the error rate of the T-1 multiplexers increases, it is to flash the appropriate link on the network map. Figure 9.2 shows an example of an application interface that associates MIB objects with map elements.

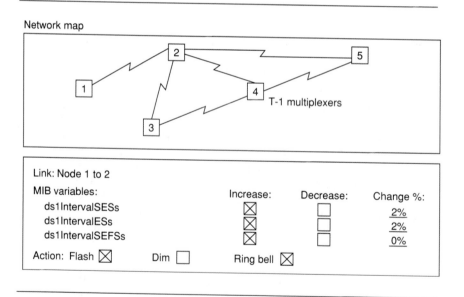

FIGURE 9.2
A network map and an application to associate T-1 specific objects to a graphical element.

[1]The T-1 is RFC 1232, titled *Definition of Managed Objects for the DS1 Interface Type*. The attribute for Severely Errored Seconds is ds1IntervalSESs.

MIB BROWSER

Once the network management system can use a MIB, you might find it helpful to have a means of browsing the MIB. A *MIB browser* shows the various groups in the MIB in a graphical manner, such as by displaying the MIB tree, and can search for MIB information about a specific function. For example, you can use a mouse to traverse the MIB tree and examine the individual objects. Or, you might want to know what area of the MIB has information about error rates. In this case, by typing in the string "errors", you could prompt the browser to show all objects on this subject. This feature of the browser is similar to having an index for the MIB. A sample browser is shown in Fig. 9.3.

MIB ALIASES

Once you have found the important objects from the new MIB, you might find it useful to associate the actual object name to a more familiar string. The *MIB alias tool* can provide this function. For example, in RFC 1213 in the interfaces table there is an object named ifInOctets. This object counts the number of octets

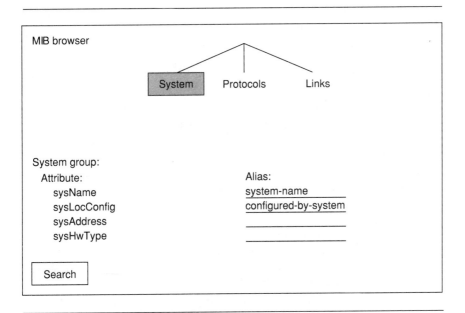

FIGURE 9.3
A MIB browser.

received in this interface. Now, an *octet* is a byte, so this object is actually counting the number of bytes input on the interface. However, because the association of octet with byte may not be obvious from the object name, the system allows you to associate this name to something that is more meaningful to you. In other words, you assign the term octet with an alias, perhaps the name Total-Input-Bytes, which might make more sense to the average user. The MIB browser allows you to alias an object that has been selected via the mouse.

MIB QUERIES

After browsing the MIB and setting up aliases, you next would probably want to look at the actual values returned by the agent on the network device. Often, the description of an object in a MIB may be vague or need clarification. One way to clarify an ambiguity is to actually query the device agent for objects from the new MIB and then examine the result. Therefore, MIB tools should include a means of allowing you to perform a one-time query of a specific MIB object. By doing this, you can know if the information the agent returns is relevant to the current task.

An extension of this facility would allow you to create your own custom MIB queries. A *custom query* is a collection of specific MIB object found in any MIB the system understands. The custom query is intended to retrieve specific information from a device that the network management system either does not show or displays in a format you would like to change. Using a custom query you create your own view of MIB objects.

There are two common methods for building the custom query: pseudo-code language and window-based generation. The pseudo-code method allows you to build a file that contains commands for building the custom query. The advantage of this method is that it is usually easy to make a single custom query and then copy it for making other queries rapidly. Its disadvantage is that you have to learn the pseudo-code language and syntax.

Using a window-based generation facility to build the custom query has two advantages: First, you don't have to learn pseudo-code and second, you can obtain immediate feedback regarding how the output of the query will appear. In this method, you are presented with a blank window. Query genera-tion is performed through by walking through menus and using a mouse to specify where on the window the output will go. For example, you could select MIB objects with the MIB browser and then denote where their output should appear on a blank window representing the custom query. The primary disad-vantage of this method is that you usually have to traverse many menus to produce the custom query.

In an example of using custom MIB queries, suppose the MIB for a workstation by the vendor *Station4Me!* allows you to query the agent for the number of users who are logged in and the processing time for their current session. Because this is *Station4Me!*- specific MIB information, the network management system does not have a standard window for viewing this information. To resolve this problem, you could build a custom query that displays the necessary information. Thereafter, you could use the custom query to learn the number of users and processing time for their current session on any *Station4Me!* workstation.

9.2 Presentation Tools

The presentation of information to the network engineer is a crucial function of a network management system. Many applications on the system attempt to present their information in an easy-to-understand manner. Still, the following presentation tools, which all applications can use, can help increase overall system productivity:

1. A centralized log for all system messages and network events that can provide you with a means of tracking network activity as seen by the system

2. A report generation tool that can enable you to specifically format the data into a text report

3. A graphics package to enable you to view data in a graphical format. This package could be offered by the system or via an interface to an existing graphics packages and would be able to present information in the common graph formats of line, bar, and pie.

CENTRALIZED LOG

A centralized log tool would show messages generated by the various applications and provide you with one location for monitoring system status. This tool would obtain its input both from the applications running on the network management system and from the network itself. If an application were to find a significant event, it could make an entry in the log, either automatically or as prompted by you.

Determination of whether an event is significant would depend on the application. For example, the fault management application that polls devices to determine their current connectivity most likely would consider the loss of communication to a device a significant event and would automatically make an entry regarding the event in the central log. On the other hand, the performance management tool that monitors statistics and thresholds could be set up so that you determine if the crossing of a threshold is an event worthy of a log entry.

This log also could show network events such as the receipt of an unsolicited message (i.e., a SNMP Trap) or the loss of connectivity to a device obtained through polling. An additional feature the centralized log tool should provide is a means for searching for specific events. The searching ability should provide a way for you to search for events between two specified time periods, as illustrated in Fig. 9.4.

As we saw in Chapter 3, "Storing Information," the network management system could use a ASCII file or relational database to store the central log. Either or both storage facilities could be useful for keeping the log information. Ideally, this would be a configurable option of the centralized log tool.

REPORT WRITER

A report writer tool would allow you to produce custom reports. Although other tools on the system will produce their own reports, you might want to produce a specific report for the network that is not available from the default system. A useful tool could be one that provides a general facility to extract data from the database using SQL and then generate reports based on that data. Thus the report format you specify could contain any valid SQL statement, including mathematical formulas. The tool further could allow you to generate reports at a given time of day, week, month, or year.

You would need to tell the report writer tool what information to extract from the database and how to display it in the report. One way for the tool to

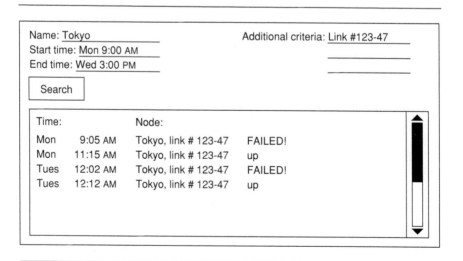

FIGURE 9.4
A sample central log tool and a specific search.

accept this input would be through a graphical interface. For example, you could be given a blank template and then use the mouse and keyboard to specify text and information retrieved from the database, as illustrated in Fig. 9.5. Using this method would allow you to see exactly what the report will look like before generation. This method is similar to that described previously for the window-based generation of custom MIB queries.

As we saw in Chapter 5, a common performance management report shows link utilization for the peak network usage times. You could set up the report writer to create a report displaying circuit names, bandwidth, and percent utilization. For full duplex serial links, *percent utilization* is a mathematical SQL formula that takes the larger of bytes in or bytes out for a given time period, converts the bytes to bits, and divides the bits by the bandwidth of the link in bits per second. In this case, you might want the system to generate this report early each morning to show the previous day utilizations.

Line utilization:

Link:
SELECT name FROM links

Bandwidth:
SELECT bw FROM links

Percent utilization:
SELECT (max (bytes-in, bytes-out) *8)
/bw FROM links

FIGURE 9.5
A sample line utilization report showing link names, bandwidth, and percent utilization. The engineer formats the report and selects the variables to retrieve from the database. From this information, the report writer generates the desired output.

GRAPHICS PACKAGE

A generic graphics package can provide another way to present information. Many tools in most functional areas of network management benefit from having a graphics package for displaying data. Like the report writer, this package would retrieve information stored in the database and allow you to produce any desired graph. The graphics package should be able to produce the three common graph types—line, bar, and pie.

This package ideally would operate by showing you a graph on the screen, enabling you to use the mouse to delineate a section of the graph, and then producing another graph of only the delineated section. The package further should allow you to alter the graph, such as changing the color of the different plots or the labels or scaling of axes.

Further, the graphics package should be able to save a snapshot of any graph in a format understood by the report writer, thus allowing reports to be generated that contain both text and graphs.

9.3 Problem-solving Tools

Intelligent problem-solving tools on the network management system can improve your productivity by tracking outstanding problems and guiding you toward problem resolution. The first of these tools, a trouble-tracking system, would allow you to track problems from discovery to resolution. The second, an expert system, would go further and, using a set of rules in combination with data about the network, could form evaluations and suggestions to help you resolve network problems. Even more advantageously, the ideal expert system could learn from previous problems and hence alter its rule base as needed.

TROUBLE-TRACKING SYSTEMS

A trouble-tracking system can monitor problems and open issues on the network that pertain not only to fault management but to all aspects of network management. For example, the system could track configuration changes, security modifications, performance requests and improvements, and accounting resources.

The system would operate by creating a new ticket for each unique problem or issue. On each ticket would be recorded the data regarding the problem or issue and the actions taken toward handling it, start to finish. Or, you or a network operator could create a ticket manually by entering all the known information about a problem. Certain information, such as the device name, the areas of the network affected, the person who administers the device, and so forth usually would be required to initiate a new ticket.

Alternatively, if possible, the network management system could fill in this information. This action would be initiated by a network event reported by a management tool; for example, as we saw in Chapter 3, sophisticated fault management tools can take steps toward solving problems. Expert systems, described later in this section, also can help the system automatically work toward problem resolution. However, if the system was not able to resolve the problem, a trouble ticket would be created that stated the problem and included the necessary information (device name, contact person, etc.) obtained from the relational database.

After the system created a ticket, the ticket would be assigned to a network engineer. Assigning tickets helps ensure problems are balanced fairly among engineers. Although the system could assign the problems automatically, but most organizations probably prefer to manually assign them because some engineers could have previous knowledge of particular problems or are better-suited for certain types of tasks. Also, if problems are assigned by the system, it could be cumbersome to inform the system whenever an engineer takes a vacation or leaves the office for a few hours; failure to do this, however, could mean the system would assign a problem to an absent engineer.

Each problem assigned to an engineer should have a classification that is entered automatically by the system or manually by an engineer. This classification can help you in the future when you are trying to categorize the problems that occur frequently. Some common classifications include link fault, network device fault, security breach, configuration error, performance problem, and accounting issue. A sample ticket entry is shown in Fig. 9.6.

The trouble-tracking system would store all information about tickets in the relational database. Doing this would allow you to browse the database for past problems that might relate to current issues. This browsing facility would need to be easy to use and should allow you to initiate an SQL search of the database using SQL based upon keywords that you enter. For example, you might enter into the system the keywords "Paris", "London", and "circuit 123-654-3432" to search for past experiences about the circuit between Paris and London on circuit number 123-654-3432. The system then would perform the necessary SQL searches and produce a listing of all past tickets matching the given criteria.

A system that generated tickets automatically also could search the system database for similar problems. Including this feature in the tool would mean that you would receive not only the ticket but also a list of past problems that are similar to the current one, data that you can use for problem solving.

The trouble-tracking system further could use the searching ability of the database to gather data on the frequency and type of past problems. This information then could be fed to the report writer, thus making available reports that list how many problems in the past were due to a particular problem with a link fault, security breach, devices by a certain vendor, etc. It also would be possible to generate a report of which problems consume the time and resources

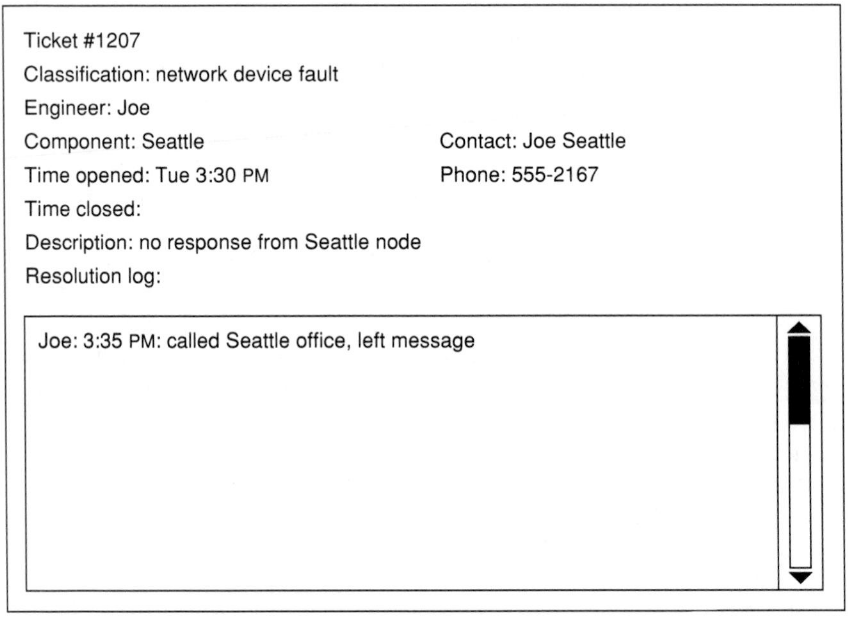

Ticket #1207
Classification: network device fault
Engineer: Joe
Component: Seattle   Contact: Joe Seattle
Time opened: Tue 3:30 PM   Phone: 555-2167
Time closed:
Description: no response from Seattle node
Resolution log:

Joe: 3:35 PM: called Seattle office, left message

FIGURE 9.6
A trouble ticket.

of network engineers. Further, you could use the graphics package to produce graphs showing this same data.

For example, suppose you have upgraded the hardware of a network device, *Opus,* which is a front-end processor to a mainframe, *Milo* (see Fig. 9.7). Although this upgrade is hardware alone, it also requires that software on *Milo* be reconfigured. Therefore, two tickets would be entered into the system outlining two problems: the hardware configuration change of *Opus* and the software configuration change necessary on *Milo.* The first ticket is classified "hardware upgrade," the second "configuration change." As engineers worked to solve these problems, they would record on their tickets each step they took. This data then would become available to help solve future similar problems on the affected device.

EXPERT SYSTEMS

An expert system can take as input the current situation on the data network, evaluate the data, estimate the possible cause, and suggest the action necessary for resolution. It does this by using a *rule set,* basically a set of if-then-else conditions

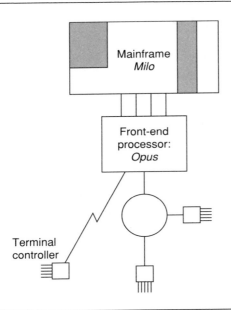

FIGURE 9.7
The front-end processor (FEP) *Opus* serves terminal controllers with users
setting up sessions with the mainframe *Milo*.

that are considered sequentially. By following these rules, the tool would be able
to draw conclusions and make suggestions given a certain set of situations. Based
on the results of this procedure, the expert system then could test some of its own
suggestions, which would eliminate the need for an engineer to perform each step
toward solving a problem.

In general, a generic set of rules can provide you with a good start toward
problem resolution. In practice, generic rules often generate not correct answers
to the problem, but generic suggestions such as "check the modems." While
these suggestions might help novice network engineers, they are of little help
to engineers who already know to perform the suggested action.

For example, if a link has failed, the expert system might know to make the
following good, generic suggestions: Check the modems at each end; check the
configuration and reachability of the network devices at each end; call the circuit
vendor. However, if the rules were more specific, such as "If circuit 123-654-3432
fails, suggest to call Allan at (415) 555-8877", the expert system would know to
check the signals on each modem or test connectivity to the network devices and
then suggest a call to the responsible network engineer. Based on the results of the
tests, the system next could use the trouble-tracking system to create a new ticket
detailing the steps the expert system has already performed.

Key to an expert system is its ability to employ past experience or historical data to alter its rule base, thus streamlining its actions to reach a correct conclusion quickly. For example, suppose there is a performance problem on a token ring. The expert system might present to you a list of possible solutions, as follows, given in order of most possible solution (see Fig. 9.8):

- Ring physically open
- Station on ring malfunctioning
- Medium attachment unit (MAU) failure
- Ring violates cable specifications

Here, we can see that the expert system would begin by evaluating each possibility on the network. It then would check each possible solution in turn and find that the first three solutions are not true. Then, it could suggest to you that the fourth possible solution—the ring is violating cable length specifications—might be the cause. Subsequently, it would open a trouble ticket for the problem.

However, you discover that the performance problem in fact results from a network device forwarding packets between the locally attached ring

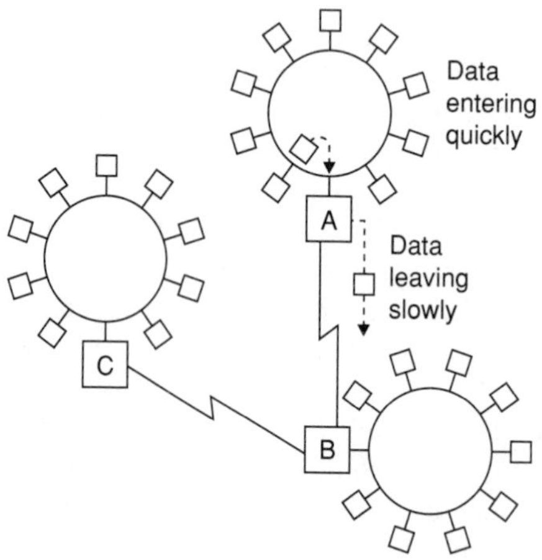

FIGURE 9.8
The slow forwarding rate of device A causes performance problems when under heavy load.

and a serial link has become overwhelmed with traffic on the ring. The network device cannot forward frames as fast as the ring can pass them, thus causing the performance problems. You then could enter the solution—upgrade the network device—into the trouble ticket. This information also would be entered into the expert system in a format that allows it to alter its own rule set. Consequently, the next time a performance problem occurred on this ring, the expert system would cycle through the first three checks given above and then try to test the performance of the network device before issuing a trouble ticket. If the network device were the problem in this subsequent performance problem, the expert system would have the correct solution and could point you directly to the answer.

While expert systems hold considerable promise for solving routine problems for network engineers, even with today's technology, they can perform relatively slowly and take a fair amount of time to run a simple test and draw conclusions. In most environments, a proficient network engineer often can be on the way to solving a problem well before an expert system offers a suggestion. When advances in the technology allow for complex expert systems to be quick and efficient, they could very well influence the engineer's job in all facets of network management.

Summary

Productivity tools can help the network engineer in a variety of ways. Three types of tools are available: MIB tools, presentation tools, and problem-solving tools. MIB tools enable an engineer to use all possible agents on the network. Presentation tools provide methods by which the engineer can display—as logs, reports, and graphs—information gathered by the network management system. Problem-solving tools can help by tracking problems to resolution and providing system-generated "educated guesses" useful in solving problems.

MIB tools include a compiler to load MIB information into the system plus tools that allow the engineer to browse the MIB, to rename confusing object names to user-defined names that are more easily understood, and to perform single queries of network agents.

Presentation tools include a central log of files stored in a text file or database management system that can present information from all network components. Other presentation tools are a generic report writer and a graphics package.

Problem-solving tools helpful to a network engineer are a trouble-tracking system and an expert system. The trouble-tracking system assigns current problems to an engineer and allows for searching through historical information. An expert system uses a rule set to offer solutions to common network problems and is able to learn from previous solutions.

For Further Study

Nadeau, R., *Mind, Machines and Human Consciousness: Are There Limits to Artificial Intelligence?*, Contemporary Books, Chicago, Il., 1991.

Payne, E. and R. McArthur, *Developing Expert Systems: A Knowledge Engineer's Handbook For Rules and Objects*, John Wiley and Sons, Inc., New York, 1990.

Wiederhold, Gio, *Database Design*, McGraw-Hill Book Company, New York, 1983.

Obtaining RFCs

Request for Comments (RFCs) are documents to communicate ideas for development in the Internet community. Some RFCs become Internet standards.

To obtain copies of RFCs, contact Government Systems, Inc., (GSI) as follows:

Telephone:
1 (800) 365–3642
1 (703) 802–4535
1 (703) 802–8376 (FAX)

Postal Mail:
Attn: Network Information Center
14200 Park Meadow Drive, Suite 200
Chantilly, Virginia, 22021

Electronic Mail:
NIC@NIC.DDN.MIL
IPAddress: 192.112.36.5

You also can use anonymous FTP to obtain RFCs from locations throughout the world. Log in to a machine using the username *anonymous* and the password *guest*. After logging in, change directories (**cd**) to the proper directory and use the **get** command to retrieve the file you desire. To end your session, enter the **quit** command. Your session should appear similar to the following:

% ftp NIC.DDN.MIL
Connected to NIC.DDN.MIL.
Name (NIC.DDN.MIL:allan): *anonymous*
331 Guest login ok, send "guest" as password
Password:
230 Guest login ok, access restrictions apply.
ftp> **cd pub/rfc**
250 CWD command successful.
ftp> **get rfc1213.txt**
ftp> **quit**
%

Following are some of the machines where you can find RFCs:

- NIC.DDN.MIL
- FTP.NISC.SRI.COM
- NIS.NSF.NET
- NISC.JVNC.NET
- WUARCHIVE.WUSTL.EDU
- VENERA.ISI.EDU
- ftp.diku.dk
- funet.fi
- mcsun.eu.net
- sunic.sunet.se
- ungle.unit.no

B

Obtaining Technical
Standards

The International Organization for Standardization (ISO), International Telephone and Telegraph Consultative Committee (CCITT), and Institute of Electrical and Electronic Engineers (IEEE) publish networking standards and recommendations. You can obtain these standards, usually for a fee, from several organizations by postal mail.

To obtain copies of ISO standards, contact the American National Standards Institute (ANSI) at the following mailing address:

1430 Broadway
New York, New York 10018
(212) 642–4932 and (212) 302–1286

To obtain copies of IEEE standards, contact the IEEE at the following mailing address:

IEEE Computer Society Press
Customer Service Center

10662 Los Vaqueros Circle
P.O. Box 3014
Los Alamitos, CA 90720–1264
(714) 821–8380

Various private organizations also offer copies of many standards. Two such organizations are the following:

Global Engineering Documents
2805 McGaw Avenue
Irvine, CA 92714
1 (800) 854–7179

Omnicom/Phillips Publishing Incorporated
P.O. Box 59665
7811 Montrose Road
Potomac, MD 20854
1 (800) OMNICOM

Glossary

A

abstract syntax   A data structure description that does not depend on hardware structures and encodings.

access point   A piece of network hardware or software that allows access to the data network.

accounting management   The process of gathering statistics about resources on the network, establishing metrics, checking quotas, determining costs, and billing network clients.

ACSE (Association Control Service Element)   The application service element that handles association establishment and release.

address   The location of a network device or service, for example, an IP address or socket for a program.

address resolution   The process of mapping one address to another (i.e., ARP) or a name to an address (i.e., name resolution).

agent   A set of software in a network device that is responsible for handling requests by a particular protocol, such as SNMP.

alarm   A sound or message used to grab the attention of a network engineer.

alert   See **alarm.**

algorithm   A method used to solve a problem.

anonymous FTP (anonymous File Transfer Protocol)   A subset of the FTP program that allows users limited access to certain files and commands.

ANSI (American National Standards Institute)   The body within the United States that coordinates voluntary standards groups.

Apple Appletalk   A network protocol suite used primarily by Apple, Inc., computers.

application   A software package, such as a network management system or tool, distinct from system software.

Application Layer   The seventh layer of the ISO Reference Model; responsible for application communication.

architecture   The method or style used in building an object, such as the software of a network management system or hardware of a network device.

ARP (Address Resolution Protocol)   A protocol for mapping IP addresses to Ethernet/IEEE 802.2 addresses; documented in RFC 826.

ASCII (American National Standard Code for Information Interchange)   A seven-bit character set used for information exchange.

ASN.1 (Abstract Syntax Notation One)   The OSI language for describing abstract syntax.

ATM (Automated Teller Machine)   A machine that performs certain banking and credit card transactions, such as cash withdrawals.

audit trail   User activity recorded for review as part of discovering security breaches.

authentication   The process of establishing the identity of a network user.

auto-discovery   A method used by a network management system to dynamically find the devices attached to a data network.

autonomous system   The piece of a data network usually under the control of a single organization and that usually runs a single interior routing protocol.

availability   The percentage of time the data network is accessible for use and operational.

B

bandwidth   The rate at which information is transmitted.

Banyan Vines   A network protocol suite used by personal computers running the operating system from Banyan, Inc.

baud rate   The number of bits per second that can be transmitted.

billing   The process of charging users for the use of the data network and its associated services.

bit   A unit of information that denotes one of two possible states, true or false; represented by a 1 or 0.

bitmapped display   A computer screen capable of setting the characteristics of each bit displayed.

bps (bits per second)   The number of bits transmitted in 1 second.

bridge   A network device that operates at the Data Link Layer and connects LANs.

brouter   A network device that performs both bridging and routing simultaneously.

buffer storage   Storage space on a network device for storing packets as they are processed or waiting to be transmitted.

byte   A series of bits treated as a single unit.

C

capacity planning   The process of determining the future requirements of network resources.

carrier signal   A continuous wave that is modulated with information on a serial connection.

CCITT (International Telephone and Telegraph Consultative Committee)
An international organization that defines standards and recommendations for the connection of telephone equipment.

centralized architecture   An architecture centered around one system.

centralized log   A storage location where all the tools and applications on the network management record information.

channel   A communication path.

channel bank   Terminal equipment for a transmission system used to multiplex individual circuits.

circuit   A communications link between two or more points.

client   A system that uses the services of a server.

cluster controller   A network device used to connect terminals to a mainframe computer.

CMIPM (Common Management Information Protocol Machine)   Software services that accept CMIS operations and initiate the appropriate procedures to accomplish the associated operation.

CMIS/CMIP (Common Management Information Services/Common Management Information Protocol)   The OSI network management services and protocol.

CMISE (Common Management Information Service Element)   An application service element responsible for deciphering the meaning of network management protocol information.

CMISE-service-user   An application that performs network management using the CMIS services.

CMOL (Common Management Information Services and Protocol over IEEE 802 Logical Link Control)   A network management protocol that implements CMIS services directly on top of the IEEE 802 Logical Link Layer. CMOL is now known as LMMP.

CMOT (Common Management Information Services over TCP)   An implementation of the CMIS services over TCP; documented in RFC 1189.

community string   An ASCII string used for authentication by SNMP.

computer server   A computer that performs processing for client computers.

concentrator node   A network device that connects many subsidiary network devices.

configuration management   The process of obtaining information from network devices and using it to manage their setup.

congestion   The point at which time bandwidth utilization causes network performance problems.

connection-less   A service in which the network delivers data between two systems independent of other simultaneous communication.

CPU (Central Processing Unit)   The main piece of hardware on a system that performs data processing.

critical network event   A network event that warrants the immediate attention of a network engineer.

CSU (Channel Service Unit)   A digital interface device that connects network devices to the local digital telephone loop.

D

database   A large, multi-purpose collection of data on a system organized so that it can be retrieved, searched, and updated rapidly.

datagram   A piece of data sent to a network that provides connection-less service.

Data Link Layer   The second layer of the ISO Reference Model; responsible for addressing, transmission, error detection, and framing on a channel.

data network   A communications network made of network devices for the purposes of transferring data between systems.

DBMS (Database Management System)   See **database.**

DEC   Digital Equipment Corporation.

de-encryption   The process of deciphering an encrypted message.

DES (Data Encryption Standard)   The standard cryptographic algorithm developed by the U.S. National Bureau of Standards.

destination host   The host that is the destination of a transaction.

device   A system that can access a data network. See **host, system**.

digit   A number between 0 and 9 inclusive.

Digital DECnet   A protocol suite used primarily by computers developed and supported by the Digital Equipment Corporation.

diskless client   A system that does not have any local storage facility and relies entirely on the network to connect to a file server.

distributed architecture   An architecture spread between many systems.

DoD (Department of Defense)   A branch of the United States government responsible for the nation's defense; responsible for developing the DOD protocols, such as TCP/IP.

DS-1 (Digital System 1)   An abbreviation used to denote the 1.44 Mbps (U.S.) or 2.108 Mbps (Europe) digital signal carried on a T-1 facility.

DS-3 (Digital System 3)   An abbreviation used to denote the 44 Mbps digital signal carried on a T-3 facility.

DSU (data service unit)   A device used in digital transmission for connecting a CSU to a network device.

E

EGP (exterior gateway protocol)   A routing protocol for passing reachability information between autonomous systems; documented in RFC 904.

electronic mail   A software service that allows one user to send a message to another user.

encryption   The scrambling of data through the use of an algorithm.

encryption key   A piece of information that serves as a basis for encryption.

enterprise network   A data network that serves an entire enterprise and its associated telecommunication needs.

entity   Any system on the network that has an SNMP agent.

Ethernet   A networking protocol developed originally by Xerox Corporation for use on LANs.

event   An occurrence on the data network that might warrant the attention of a network engineer.

expert system   A system that has the ability to learn and aids in problem solving by using a rule-based system.

F

fault   A problem on the data network.

fault management   The process of identifying network faults, isolating the cause of the fault, and if possible, correcting the fault.

FDDI (Fiber Distributed Data Interface)   A standard specifying a 100 Mbps token-passing network using fiber-optic cable.

FEP (Front-End Processor)   A network device that provides network interface capabilities for a network device.

fiber-optic cable   A network medium that conducts modulated light transmission.

file   An ordered collection of data.

file server   A system with disk space used by multiple clients.

file system   The storage space on a host.

file transfer   An application that moves files from one network device to another.

filter   A process that limits information based on certain criteria.

finger   An application that allow users to learn if other users are logged into the local and remote systems.

firefighting   A situation in which network engineers spend most of their time continually solving problems and not working toward the future development of the data network.

flow control   A technique for ensuring a transmitting host does not overrun a receiving host with data.

fragment   A piece of a packet that has been broken into smaller units.

FTP (File Transfer Protocol)   An IP application protocol for transferring files between network devices.

full duplex   A capability for the simultaneous transmission of data in both directions.

G

gateway   A network device that can perform protocol conversion from one protocol stack to another.

graph   Method used to display data in a pictorial manner, such in a bar, line, or pie shape.

graphical user interface   The user interface to an application that uses graphics instead of only text.

graphics package   A package that converts data into graphs.

H

half-duplex   The capability of transmitting data in one direction at a time.

hardware   The physical components of a computer.

hardware address   A Data Link Layer address for a network device. See **MAC address, physical address.**

HEMS (High-Level Entity Management System)   A network management protocol that was considered for Internet standardization; documented in RFC 1076.

hop count   A routing metric used to find the distance between two network devices.

host   A computer system on a data network. See **device, system.**

host authentication   A process whereby the destination host identifies the source host of a transaction by its name or address.

hub   A network device that is the center of a star-topology network.

I

IAB (Internet Activities Board)   A group that oversees the work in networking technology and protocols for the TCP/IP internetworking community.

IBM   International Business Machines.

IBM SNA (IBM Systems Network Architecture)   A network architecture developed by IBM.

ICMP (Internet Control Message Protocol)   A network layer protocol that carries messages to report errors relevant to IP packet processing; documented in RFC 792.

IEEE (Institute of Electrical and Electronic Engineers)   A professional organization that defines network standards.

IETF (Internet Engineering Task Force)   A subgroup of the IAB chartered to identify and coordinate solutions in the areas of management, engineering, and operations of the Internet.

interface   A connection between two network devices or hosts.

Internet   A term used to refer to the world's largest internetwork, which connects thousands of networks around the world.

internetwork   A collection of networks interconnected by network devices that generally act as a single network.

Internet worm   A program written by Robert Morris, Jr., that used various techniques to spread itself throughout the Internet in November 1988.

inventory   An itemized list of current items, such as network devices.

IP (Internet protocol)   A Network Layer protocol that contains addressing and control information for packets to be routed; documented in RFC 791.

IRTF (Internet Research Task Force)   A subgroup of the IAB chartered to work on research problems concerning the TCP/IP network community and the Internet.

ISO (International Organization for Standardization)   An international body that develops, suggests, and names standards for network protocols.

ISO Reference Model   A network architectural model developed by the ISO and CCITT; used universally for understanding and teaching network functionality.

K

Kbps (Kilobits per second)   One thousand bits per second.

Kerberos   The implementation of a key authentication service written by MIT Project Athena.

key   A unique piece of information in a packet that authenticates the data in a transaction.

key authentication   A process whereby the destination host requires the source host of a transaction to present a key for the transaction.

key server   A server that validates requests for transactions between hosts by giving out keys.

L

labeled node   A piece of information in the MIB tree that has an object identifier and a short text description.

LAN (Local Area Network)   A high-speed network covering a limited geographic area, such as a single building.

leased line   A transmission line set up by a communications carrier for the private use of a customer.

link   A communications channel between source and destination and including all intervening network devices.

link driver   A network device that ensures reliable transmissions of digital signals over long distances.

LLC (Logical Link Control)   An IEEE sub-layer of the Data Link Layer that handles framing, flow control, and errors.

LMMP (LAN Man Management Protocol)   A network management protocol formerly known as CMOL that implements CMIS services on top of IEEE 802 Logical Link Layer for use in LAN environments.

log file   A file that maintains a record of information output by applications and that may be useful for later examination.

LPP (Lightweight Presentation Protocol)   A protocol on the ISO Presentation Layer that does not provide the full functionality of the complete ISO Presentation Layer, thus making it easier to implement; documented in RFC 1085.

M

MAC (Media Access Control)   The lower portion of the Data Link Layer as defined by IEEE; concerned with media access issues.

MAC address   A Data Link Layer address for a network device. See **physical address, hardware address.**

mainframe   A large computing system.

managed object   A network device that can be managed by a network management protocol.

management association service   A class of CMIS services that controls the interaction between peer open systems.

management notification service   A class of CMIS services that provides information about network events.

management operation service   A class of CMIS services that provides the ability to manage network devices.

MAU (Medium Attachment Unit for IEEE 802.3; Multistation Access Unit for IEEE 802.5)   In IEEE 802.3, a Physical Layer network device that performs collision detection and the transfer of bits to and from the network. In IEEE 802.5, a wiring concentrator that attaches multiple stations to the network.

Mbps (Megabits per second)   Ten thousand bits per second.

media   The physical substance through which pass transmission signals such as coaxial or fiber optic cable.

message   A logical collection of information in the Application Layer.

MIB (Management Information Base)   A database of managed objects accessed by network management protocols.

MIB-I (Management Information Base I)   The first MIB defined for managing TCP/IP-based internets; documented in RFC 1156.

MIB-II (Management Information Base II)   The current standard MIB defined for managing TCP/IP-based internets; documented in RFC 1213.

microwave link   A communications link based upon electromagnetic waves.

MIT   Massachusetts Institute of Technology.

modem (modulator-demodulator)   A device that performs bi-directional conversion from digital signals into a form for communication over analog communication facilities.

MTBF (Mean Time Between Failures)   The average time between failures of an object, such as a network device.

MTU (Maximum Transmission Unit)   The maximum size of a packet (in bytes) that can be handled over an interface.

multiplexer   A network device used to switch circuits.

N

name resolution   The process of resolving a system name to a network address through the use of a name server.

name server   A system that responds to queries to map system names to network addresses.

network   See **data network.**

network access point   A location, such as a port or software program, by which users obtain access to the network.

network address   A Network Layer address that refers to a logical, not physical, network device.

network billing   The process of billing users of a data network to recover expenses or obtain profit.

network component   See **network device.**

network device   A generic term referring to any device that can access a network.

network engineer   A person responsible for one or more of the following tasks on a data network: installation, maintenance, and troubleshooting.

network inventory   A collection of information about network devices, circuit, people, vendors, and so forth useful for accomplishing network management.

Network Layer   The third layer of the ISO Reference Model; handles routing.

network management   The task of controlling a complex data network so that it can be used in an useful and proficient manner. Network management is divided into five categories: fault management, configuration management, security management, performance management, and accounting management.

network management architecture   The architecture of a network management system describing the framework for applications that perform network management.

network management protocol   A protocol designed to perform network management.

network management system   A bundle of software that provides features and functionality to help network engineers.

network operator   A person who helps performs tasks to help operate the network on a day-to-day basis.

network protocol   A protocol that operates at the Network Layer.

network resource   A network device that provides a service for users.

network simulation   The process of simulating how a network will act and perform.

network topology   The physical arrangement of network devices and media with a data network.

NIC (Network Information Center)   A center that serves the Internet community by providing user assistance, documentation, and other services.

node   See **network device.**

Novell IPX (Novell Internetwork Packet Exchange)   A network protocol suite used by personal computers running the operating system from Novell, Inc.

O

object   A piece of information in a MIB tree that is either an intermediary node or leaf node containing a value.

OID (object identifier)   A series of integers separated by periods that denote the exact traversal of a MIB tree to a labeled node.

open system   A system running the OSI protocol stack.

operating system   The application, such as UNIX or DOS, on a computer that performs intrinsic functions such as file and storage system access.

operating system security   The security mechanisms within an operating system that limit the actions of users and protect information.

OSI (Open Systems Interconnection)   An international network protocol suite developed by ISO and CCITT for use on multivendor equipment.

P

packet   A logical collection of data.

packet filter   A configuration in a network device that limits the flow of a packet based on certain criteria.

password   A series of characters that uniquely identifies a user.

PC (Personal Computer)   A computer system, such as an IBM PC or Apple Macintosh, used by a single user.

performance management   The process of analyzing the characteristics of a data network to monitor and increase its efficiency.

physical address   The Data Link Layer address of a network device. See **hardware address, MAC address.**

Physical Layer   The first layer of the ISO Reference Model; defines the mechanical, physical, and electrical interface to a network and its associated medium.

physical security   The physical security of network devices, such as locked doors and keyboards.

polling   The process whereby one device queries other devices for information.

port   An interface to a networking device.

Presentation Layer   The sixth layer of the ISO Reference Model; controls the syntax of information passed between two Application Layer programs.

print server   A system with a printer used by multiple clients.

protocol   A formal description of a set of rules and conventions that describe how network devices exchange information.

protocol analyzer   A network device used to capture packets on a network and analyze their contents.

protocol translator   A network device or software package that converts one protocol into another.

proxy agent   An agent that can gather information about other systems and then relay this information to a management station via a protocol, such as SNMP.

public data network   A network set up by a government or private organization to provide widespread communications to the public, sometimes for a fee.

Q

query   A message that inquires of the status of an object or device.

quota   The amount of a network resources allowed for a user or group.

R

RAM (Random Access Memory)   A type of computer memory in which the access time is independent of the address.

RDBMS (Relational Database Management System)   A database that allows for relationships to be made between data.

reachability   The process of establishing if one system can communicate with another.

rejection rate   The amount of time a network cannot transfer information because of a lack of resources and performance.

remote bridge   A bridge that connects physically separate network segments via a WAN link.

remote login   An application allowing users to log in to a system via the network.

repeater   A Physical Layer network device that regenerates and propagates bits between two network segments.

reports   Text, and possible graphics, showing the results of a process or the listing of numerical information.

report writer   A set of software tools that helps in the writing and formatting of reports.

response time   The amount of time it takes for a piece of information to enter the network and be processed and then have a response leave the network.

RFC (Request For Comments)   Documents to communicate ideas for development in the Internet community and that might become Internet standards.

ROM (Read Only Memory)   A type of computer memory that can be read but not changed.

ROSE (Remote Operations Service Element)   An OSI application protocol used to access remote open systems.

route   The path between two systems on a data network.

router   A network device that can decide how to forward packets through a network by examining Network Layer information.

RTT (Round-Trip Time)   The time required for information to travel from the source system, through all intermediate network devices, to the destination system, and back to the source system.

S

satellite link   A link that uses geostationary orbiting satellites to provide communications links between two network devices.

SDLC (Synchronous Data Link Control)   An IBM synchronous Data Link Layer protocol used on serial links.

security management   The process of protecting access to sensitive information found on systems attached to a data network.

security violation   A breach in security that results in unauthorized users accessing sensitive information.

sendmail   A UNIX application that provides electronic mail service through the use of SMTP.

sensitive information   Any data on a system that an organization decides to secure, such as business data, customer information, and research and development schedules.

serial interface   A network interface that connects to a serial link.

serial link   A link in which the bits of a data character are transmitted, in order, over a single channel.

server   A generic term used to refer to a host that offers some service to client hosts.

session   A related set of communications transactions between two network devices.

Session Layer   The fifth layer of the ISO Reference Model; coordinates session activity between applications, such as remote procedure calls.

SGMP (Simple Gateway Monitoring Protocol)   A network management protocol that was considered for Internet standardization and later evolved into SNMP; documented in RFC 1028.

SMI (Structure of Management Information)   Rules used to define managed objects in a MIB; documented in RFC 1155.

SMTP (Simple Mail Transfer Protocol)   An Internet protocol providing electronic mail services.

SNMP (Simple Network Management Protocol)   A network management protocol used for managing IP network devices; documented in RFC 1157.

socket   A software data structure that provides a communications access point within a network device.

software   A set of computer programs.

source host   The host that is the source of a transaction.

source route bridge   A network device that performs source routing in a situation in which the entire route to a destination is predetermined prior to sending data.

spanning tree   A subset of a network topology without loops.

spanning tree algorithm   An algorithm for preventing loops in a bridged network through the use of a spanning tree.

SQL (Structured Query Language)   A standard language developed by ANSI for accessing databases.

SQL query   A request for information within a database using SQL.

standard   An officially specified or commonly used collection of rules or procedures.

subnet mask   A 32-bit address mask used in IP to calculate a specific subnet.

system   A generic term used to describe a network device or computer on a data network. See **host.**

T

T-1   A telephony term to describe a digital carrier facility for the transmission of data at 1.544 Mbps.

T-3   A digital WAN service that provides transmission of data at 44 Mbps.

TCP (Transport Control Protocol)   A Transport Layer protocol that provides reliable transmission of data on IP networks; documented in RFC 793.

TCP/IP   The two most popular Internet protocols that provide Transport Layer and Network Layer service.

technology   A method or process for handling a technical problem.

telecommunications   A generic term describing communications over a telephone network and that involve computer systems.

terminal   A computer device that can display text and graphics but that has no processing power.

terminal server   A network device that connects asynchronous devices to a WAN or LAN.

text message   A message or other output that does not require graphics for viewing, such as a line of text on a ASCII terminal.

TFTP (Trivial File Transfer Protocol)   A simplified version of FTP that performs the transfer of files from one host to another (usually without the use of a password); documented in RFC 783.

threshold   A point at which time a significant event may occur.

throughput   The rate of information arriving at, and possibly going through, a point in a network system.

timeout   An event that happens when one network device expects to hear from another within a specified amount of time, but does not.

token ring   A communications process that produces a result.

Transport Layer   The fourth layer of the ISO Reference Model; responsible for reliable network communication between hosts.

trap   Unsolicited message sent by an SNMP agent to a management station to alert about a specific network event.

trend analysis   An analysis of information over a period of time with an emphasis on predicting future data points.

troubleshooting   The process of diagnosing and fixing problems.

trouble-tracking system   A software package designed to help network engineers track the resolution of current and past network problems.

twisted-pair   A transmission media consisting of two insulated or non-insulated wires arranged in a regular spiral pattern.

U

UDP (User Datagram Protocol)   A connection-less transport protocol used on IP networks; documented in RFC 768.

UNIX   A popular operating system for computers.

user   A person who utilizes a network device or computer system.

user authentication   A process whereby the destination host uniquely identifies the source user of a transaction, usually through the use of a password.

user interface   The interface the user sees when communicating with a software tool or application.

utilization   The amount of use of a network device, link, or system.

V

vendor   An organization that sells network devices or systems.

virtual circuit   A logical circuit established to produce reliable communication between two network devices.

W

WAN (Wide Area Network)   A data network that spans a large geographic area.

wiring closet   A room designed for data and voice networks that often serves as a central location for network devices.

workstation   A mid-sized computer system designed for a small number of users.

X

X11   See **X Window System.**

X.25   A CCITT standard that specifies packet format for the transfer of data in a public data network.

X.400   A CCITT recommendation that defines a standard for the transfer of electronic mail.

X.500   A CCITT recommendation that defines a standard for distributed maintenance of directories and files.

X Window System   A distributed windowing system that is vendor and machine independent; originally developed by MIT for UNIX workstations.

Xerox XNS (Xerox Network Systems)   A network protocol suite used by personal computers developed by Xerox PARC.

Index